PEDRO LAPA

History and Interregnum

Three Works by Stan Douglas

MUSEU COLEÇÃO BERARDO

ARCHIVE BOOKS

Since its inception, the Museu Coleção Berardo has lavished special attention upon the most significant artistic developments of our day. It is a source of profound gratification to be presenting an exhibition of Canadian artist, Stan Douglas, to be able to share his exceptional work with the public. If showing this work is testament to our appreciation of one of the most important artists of our time, there remains more to be said concerning this exhibition and the projects it incorporates. The nuances of meaning, complexity of expression and, simultaneously, the disarming power of synthesis that these three works occasion are linked to a contemplation of a specific period in the recent history of Portugal, Angola and of jazz as an expression of cultural criticism. The relations with our recent history contained in these works are sources of particular interest, not only for people like myself, who experienced the hope that these historical moments kindled, but also prompting a broader consideration concerning the construction of a new life and culture in the context of a world always constrained by the sharing of powers — at the particular time in question, those involved in the Cold War; today, no less tragically, those of globalisation.

This exhibition has been seven years in the making by Stan Douglas and our artistic director, Pedro Lapa, a project that has finally enjoyed realisation. The fact that it has taken place here in Lisbon, at the Museu Coleção Berardo, is, for me, a source of great satisfaction. I would like to congratulate Stan Douglas for his work's capacity to project the hopes held in our memories while encouraging us forward into the future.

José Berardo

Honorary President of the Board of Trustees
Fundação de Arte Moderna e Contemporânea – Coleção Berardo

The idea of making a work based on an adaptation of
Joseph Conrad's *The Secret Agent* had, for a long while,
been one that Stan Douglas had long entertained as
a future project. In 2008, following upon other collabo-
rations, I was able to invite him to make an original
work in some way linked to Lisbon. Stan undertook
preliminary research, not only fact-finding but also to
establish if there were any locations and devices that
might, as in many of his works, be amenable to articulation with an adaptation of the plot of that famous novella,
where the criminal and the political are intertwined.
Various setbacks delayed this project, until the David
Zwirner gallery generously provided the means for its
realisation in the of this feature length film conceived as
a cinematic installation. The transposition of the plot to
a situation following upon the revolution of 25 April 1974
in Portugal provided the historical and political context
elected. *The Secret Agent* was filmed in Lisbon in March
2015, with a large cast of Portuguese actors, produced by
the prestigious *O Som e a Fúria*. Indeed, the year 1975,
with its designation PREC (Revolutionary Process in
Progress) constituted, for Portuguese society, a moment
outside the axes of history, at that time still well in the
Cold War, with its immovable geopolitical boundaries.
Multiple possibilities and conjectures concerning the
course of a revolution were then played out, both within
and outside Portugal. It is to this unexpected suspension
of historical determinations, and to the attempts to appropriate that which cannot be appropriated, as well as to
the outline of the closure of this moment, that *The Secret
Agent* casts its gaze.

    As such, the exhibition *Interregnum* brings together
other recent works relating to the same period, where the
end of Portuguese colonialism, alongside other cultural

manifestations such as free jazz and afrobeat, coincides
with a multicultural, emancipatory project dreamed of at
the end of this period, but upon which a new epoch,
with new power configurations, was to superimpose itself.

Disco Angola (2012) and Luanda–Kinshasa (2013)
are works that address these questions. They were made
while Stan Douglas was researching the transformation
of Portuguese life in the decade of the 1970s, and the
emergence of a new global order. To this end, not only
the empirical witnesses to the facts alluded to, but also
the record of their subsequent historiographic or artistic
consideration, alongside the vast body of existing, and
in particular photographic, documentation, constituted
the principal sources. Stan Douglas's relation to these
aspects of the work was precise, moving from the work
to the historical details that might inform it, or exploring
the cultural context that the work probes. The re-enactments of the various situations made possible this infinite
approximation between the fiction inherent in any work
of art with the documentary material that informs it.

Pedro Lapa

History and Interregnum

On the eve of the events to which *Luanda–Kinshasa*, *The Secret Agent* and *Disco Angola* refer, an event took place that was significant with regard to expectations that were, at the time, exciting many people. These became manifest in sudden eruptions, spurred by a desire for radical change. On the night of 20 November, 1971, the first *Cascais Jazz* festival took place in the small city of Cascais, west of Lisbon. Between that date and 1980, the greatest names in the history of jazz performed here. Launching the first edition was Miles Davis, with his fusion of jazz and rock earning him immense popularity, but also a measure of criticism from the more orthodox jazz public. His performance kindled the impatience of Ornette Coleman, who performed after him, and who was somewhat piqued at being the follow-up act. With Dewey Redman, Charlie Haden and Ed Blackwell, Davis's offering was a form of arrhythmical, anti-harmonic free jazz, discussed in the reviews at the time.[1]

During their set, Charlie Haden introduced "Song for Che," dedicating it to the liberation movements of Angola and Mozambique. The audience took to its feet, clapping out a beat, fists raised. As recalled by Haden: "[...] and the pandemonium was immediate, was like everybody screaming, cheering. Almost like a riot broke out. You couldn't even hear the song we're playing."[2] At this time, Portugal was under the yoke of one of the

1   For a complete description of the episode, see http://jnpdi.blogspot. pt/2009/04/25-de-abril-e-o-jazz-antes-da-liberdade.html (consulted 10 June, 2015).
2   Statement by Charlie Haden to the programme *Diálogo em Maio – Carlos Paredes e Charlie Haden ao Vivo no Coliseu*, by Carlos Barradas (production) and João Henrique/RTP (production), Centro de Produção de Lisboa: 1991.

oldest fascist and colonial regimes in Europe. The riot
police intended to storm the stage, but was wary of the
vast public and the possibility of chairs being thrown.
At the end of the performance, Dewey Redman raised
his fist, and Charlie Haden was detained by PIDE[3] was
immediately forced to head for the Lisbon airport, and
landed up being taken the next day to the police head-
quarters for interrogation. Fortunately, the recording
that had been the cause of his detention was not found
in his raincoat pocket. Later, that recording was included
on his disc *Closeness*, of 1976, bearing the title "For a Free
Portugal." Haden was escorted by the political police
to the home of the cultural attaché of the US Embassy
in Lisbon, but it was only on the following day that he
was finally able to depart for London.

HISTORY, DISCONTINUITY AND FICTION

This short episode, taking place on the eve of the
Portuguese revolution of 1974 and of the fictional events
presented by Stan Douglas in *Luanda–Kinshasa* (2013),
The Secret Agent (2015) and *Disco Angola* (2012), is an
exemplary situation, invoking a recent past. Its example
should be considered singular,[4] since it does not express
something universal in the three works, nor is it constituted as an alien disparity. Rather, it is invoked as a singular
moment, probing, on the level of the discursive, a relation

---

3   This acronym stood for the *Polícia Internacional e de Defesa do Estado*
(the International Police and the Defence of the State), created by the dictator
António Oliveira Salazar in 1946. Its mission was the repression, using every
means (prison, torture, concentration camps), of all forms of opposition to the
fascist regime. In 1968 changed its name to DGS (Directorate of General Safety),
though in colloquial terms the original designation was never abandoned.
4   I am following the concept of "example" as defined by Giorgio
Agamben in "The Example," *The Coming Community*, transl. Michael
Hardt, Minneapolis: University of Minnesota Press, 1993.

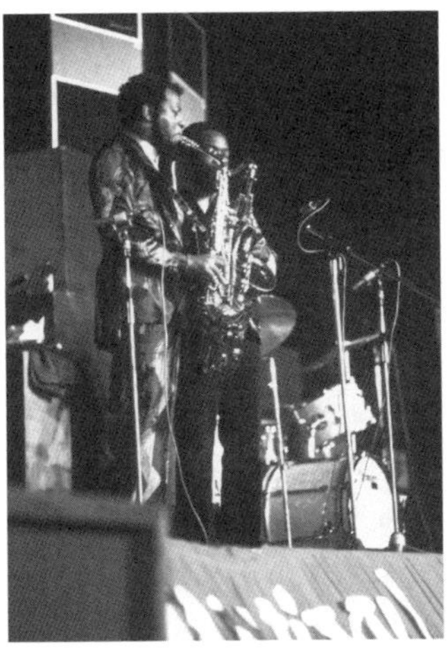

A

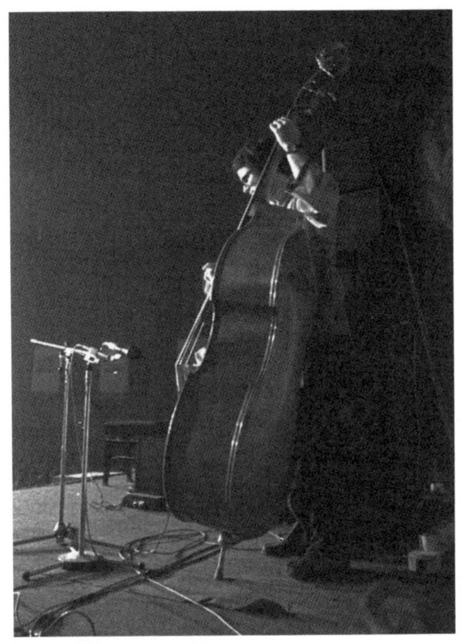

B

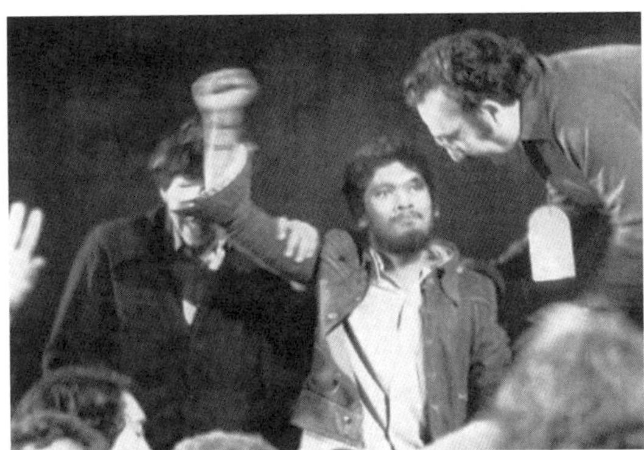

C

A   Ornette Coleman and Dewey Redman at *Cascais Jazz'71*, Cascais International Jazz Festival, 1971. Photograph by José Carlos Nascimento.
B   Charlie Haden at *Cascais Jazz'71*, Cascais International Jazz Festival, 1971. Photograph by José Carlos Nascimento.
C   Audience reacts to Charlie Haden's tribute to anti-colonial liberation movements at *Cascais Jazz'71*, Cascais International Jazz Festival, 1971. Photograph from the archives of *Diário de Lisboa*.

between the three works. It merely brings them together
in order to throw light upon a set of forces and tensions,
and thus, based on a factual episode, to narrate a temporal
sequence, culminating in the re-enactments that these
three works bring about. A new musical form, the revolution, the end of colonialism and the relations that these
conditions might establish among themselves: doubtlessly,
these are likely to generate diverse constructions and points
of view, but they are not determined by a common identity
declared by the example as a point of temporal origin.

These works are situated at the time that saw the end
of a catastrophe – this being the purpose of revolution –
when people were experiencing the euphoria of that
suspended moment, and the pervasiveness of its expression
in the discursive field; where all its possibilities inter-
communicate, giving way to a new form of givenness.
As Susan Buck-Morss has explained, it is not a question
of affirming the autonomy of the imagination in relation
to historical materialism, but rather, of grasping that
"[t]he technological capacity to produce must be mediated by the utopian capacity to dream – and vice versa."[5]

It is, indeed, from another historical time that
Stan Douglas observed that interregnum that is hinted
at by the three works in question. In *Luanda–Kinshasa,
The Secret Agent* and *Disco Angola*, anticipation has
given rise to the dispersal of singularities, to pure event,
and this becomes the focus, external to the immanence
of the intentionality of a historic subject. Stan Douglas
follows the contours of this interstitial time with an attentive gaze, stripped of nostalgia. It is only from a position
on the outside might one comprehend the conditions
of its possibility. This allusion to specific past historical
events in the majority of Stan Douglas's work, entails

---

5   Susan Buck-Morss, *The Dialectis of Seeing. Walter Benjamin and the
      Arcades Project*. Cambridge, Mass. & London: The MIT Press, 1989, p. 120.

the "potency of inactuality:"[6] this is not the negation of time, but rather, an emergence in the dialectic between the historical present of the *now*, and a return to a *then*.

Hal Foster called this concern an "archival impulse," shared by diverse artists of a particular generation across the globe. While this impulse is not a new one, its characteristics are distinctive, since this is not simply work that "draws on informal archives but produces them as well, and does so in a way that underscores the nature of all archival materials as found yet constructed, factual yet fictive, public yet private."[7] While these have all been features of Stan Douglas's work from *Overture* (1986) onwards – one might even say he has been a pioneer in this respect – in his more recent works, these features might be considered a substrate of the fictional construction that the medium mobilises. With the changes that have occurred in the field of photography and film in the digital age, found materials may be submitted to a process of montage capable of aggregating, in a fiction constructed on these supports, the most disparate elements from divergent sources, linked to a certain historical event, and at times only fragmentarily glimpsed among the diverse materials contained by the archive. This is not a process of digitally surpassing "the nature of all archival material" that Foster seems to fear as an ideological or historicist assumption, not least because

6   Giorgio Agamben, "La Puissance de la pensée", in *La Puissance de la pensée*. Paris: Éditions Payot & Rivages, 2006. In this work, Agamben undertakes a commentary on the "constitutive co-belonging of power and impotence," in relation to the "Book IX – Theta" of Aristotles' *Metaphysics*, where he states that "every potentiality is impotentiality of the same and with respect to the same." For Agamben, "the thesis thus defines the specific ambivalence of all human potentiality, in the original structure, is maintained in relation to its own privation, and is always – relative to the same – the potency to be or not to be, to make or not to make. This is the relation that constitutes, for Aristotle, the essence of potency/potentiality." Giorgio Agamben, *ibid.*, pp. 239-240. Translations mine.
7   Hal Foster, "An Archival Impulse" in *October*, 110, Fall 2004, Cambridge, Mass.: The MIT Press Journals, p. 5.

Stan Douglas has, at times, played off obsolete devices against digital ones, as he does in *Journey into Fear* (2001) or *Inconsolable Memories* (2005). On the contrary, this refers to an artistic form of construction of collective memory that contests the originary aspiration to the truth of the historical document.

To the extent that the substance of the document is constituted by verbal, imagetic or other signs, and these – in their capacity as traces of the world – are articulated as language, the document does not lose its relation to the world of actions and objects underpinning it, but is, rather, constructed, as Michel Foucault has it, as an utterance. In other words "the function that gave a series of signs (a series that is not necessarily grammatical or logically structured) an existence, and a specific existence […] An existence that reveals such a series […] as a relation to a domain of objects; […] a set of possible positions for a subject; […] an element in a field of coexistence; […] a repeatable materiality."[8] In turn, these utterances co-exist among themselves in a discursive formation that grants them a place in the processes of elaboration of the documentary material, whereby each series is no longer an immediate instrument of memory, but rather, the process of its construction. Vexation has thus become constitutive of this series. What Foucault describes is the displacement of our focus to the intentionality of any given historical subject with regard to the relations between discursive formations. Such discursive formations are not ideal or atemporal forms; rather, discourse "poses the problem of its own limits, its divisions, its transformations."[9] Thus emerges discursive practice around the documentary material, uttered from an external position, enabling us to envision the horizon of

8   Michel Foucault, *The Archaeology of Knowledge*, transl. from the French by A.M. Sheridan Smith, London: Routledge, (1972) 1997, pp. 108-109.
9   *Ibid.*, p. 117.

possibility of a given space-time that defines any epoch.[10]

It is not so much the manifest content that is relevant here, but rather, the conditions of possibility of the utterance, defined by their discursive relations and not in relation to an originary point of reference. All of this appears, to some extent, removed from Stan Douglas as he works with artistic forms. For although he often publishes the documentary material that underpins his works, or even elaborates new documentary material, as in several photographic series linked to the video or film installations, these do not present the film stills of the final work, nor do they represent situations directly linked to the action of the film.[11] Rather, they are completely autonomous, constituting a new artistic configuration based on the documentary material.[12] In this sense, the document continually recedes and tends to lose its indexical value as truth effect, to be observed from the far shore of its exteriority. By this token, the recourse to digital means allows for a penetration of documental materiality and its exposure as a bundle of signs of a historical world, offered up for reflection.[13] It is through the transposition

10   I cannot resist citing a much-quoted statement by Stan Douglas: "To a large degree, my concern is not to redeem these past events but to reconsider them: to understand why these utopian moments did not fulfil themselves, what larger forces kept a local moment a minor moment: and what was valuable there – what might still be useful today." "In conversation with Lynne Cooke" *in* Scott Watson, Diana Thater, Carol J. Clover (eds.), *Stan Douglas*. London: Phaidon, 1998, p. 116.

11   Only in his *Klatsassin: Character Portraits* (2006), Vienna Secession (catalogue published in 2008), does Stan Douglas utilize the characters of the film in order to have recourse to the genre of portraiture.

12   For an analysis of this question in the Stan Douglas' work, see Dieter Roelstraete, "Apparition theory: Stan Douglas and photography" in *Stan Douglas*. Göttingen: Steidl, 2013.

13   As Bernard Stiegler has it, this exteriorisation of the document in the digital presupposes a loss of intimacy and is constituted as a third retention, implying a mnemo-technical exteriorisation. See Bernard Stiegler, "L'économie retentionnelle" in *Pour une nouvelle critique de l'économie politique*. Paris: Galilée, 2009. However, it is in an artistic elaboration of this mnemo-technical exteriorisation that is given to us, not the intimate memory that Stiegler designates "second retention," but a critical, non-alienated possibility.

of documentary traces into signs that the works of Stan Douglas marshal, whether digitally or otherwise, their discursive formations.

More recently, Jacques Rancière has found in the problematisation of the discursive relations between history and fiction, the manifestation of fictional structure as a modality inherent to the elaboration of intelligibility for history, which is nothing if not the revelation of an "impossibility of a historic rationality." For Rancière, "to pretend is not to put forth illusions but to elaborate intelligible structures," so that it is not a question of the distinction between fiction and falsity, but a blurring of the borders "between the logic of facts and the logic of fictions *and* the new mode of rationality that characterizes the science of history."[14] If "the real must be fictionalized in order to be thought"[15] he nevertheless alerts us to the fact that it is not a matter of affirming that everything is fiction, but rather, of understanding the forms through which art reorganises the signs and images of its discursive formations. This fundamental lack of distinction between art and history, in which fiction freely circulates, emerges in the work of Stan Douglas in the most diverse configurations, of which these three works are distinct examples.

Obviously, Stan Douglas is not concerned with the creation of an effect of pure verisimilitude or pure simulacrum, both of which would entail representations that would eventually play about with the re-staged document via digital prestidigitation, disentangling the relation between historic agents and the subject of the utterance. It is from an external position that documents are approached, and the re-enactments, in these three works, of a given historical period, contrary

14 Jacques Rancière, *The Politics of Aeshtetics. The Distribution of the Sensible*, London: Continuum, 2004, p. 36.
15 *Ibid.*, p. 38.

to simulation which repositions a historical subject within the confines of an eternal repetition of the same, enables the subject to extract himself from the binds linking him to his own documentary material, closing in simultaneously on images of temporal happiness and its shadow, projecting such images as fictions for another life.

In an essay on the origins and current practices of re-enactment, Sven Lütticken asks if "in the neoliberal theater everybody constantly reenacts himself *and* indirectly everyone else as well, reenactment becomes a crucial performative strategy [...]. [O]ne might just as well use reenactment against itself by reenacting historical events. But can such a re-enactment succeed in breaking through the eternal return of the same, rather than ensuring its continuation?"[16] What a simple simulation — facilitated by technical resources — risks, is the repositioning of a context where the avatars, hierarchy and the theatre of its acts, once again under cover of the desire for a new perspective, would be able to achieve an order of history already consigned and exemplified by fiction, as a degraded substitute for facts. Out of documented and exemplary situations (and to the extent that they relate with others, while not disputing a common essentiality), Stan Douglas undertakes a re-enactment that, by the handling of its discursive substance, explores the performativity of history itself. In rigorously re-organising its signs, the fiction inherent in discourse elicits an iterative dimension from those signs, implicating, in the process, a web of interpretive suggestions that rises over and above any purely positivist wish, one that might be circumscribed by a strict verification of facts.

In this process, the re-enactment of a particular historical moment (true or fictional, with greater or lesser

16   Sven Lütticken, "An Arena in Which to Reenact" in *Life, Once More — Forms of Reenactment in Contemporary Art*. Rotterdam: Witte de With, Center for Contemporary Art, 2005, p. 19.

degree of verisimilitude with respect to a given event),
becomes the actualisation of other possibilities from
the past. This dialectic thus carries with it a potential of
repetition, one that should not be thought of as a return of
the same, but rather, as the constitution of the affirmation
of the very process of becoming, which thus returns.
Each image from the past constitutes itself in the present,
though not in the sense of a negation of another present
that would reject it as definitive past, but rather, just as a
present that constitutes itself in the past as the capacity
for another life. There is thus no definitively constituted
origin for an eternal return as the repetition of the same,
but rather, a becoming of multiplicities that return as differences. In etymologically querying Nietzsche's expression *eternal return of the same* (*ewige Wiederkehr des
Gleichen*),[17] Giorgio Agamben has shown that the word
gleich refers to the idea of image, so that what returns is
an image or a similitude, and not actually the entity itself.
Agamben comes to compare this to Walter Benjamin's
dialectic image. The return that the re-enactment brings
about might well imply a critical perspective on history,
as against historicism. Thus, what returns with the actualisation of a situation in historical time that each work
performs — in other words, with each example — is the
unfolding of singularities played in becoming, and their
respective returns, introducing a structural discontinuity
capable of breaking reproductive repetition and "stag[ing]
small but significant acts of difference."[18]

17 Giorgio Agamben, "L'image immémoriale" in *La Puissance de la pensée*.
Paris: Éditions Payot & Rivages, 2006, pp. 283-284.
18 Sven Lütticken, *op. cit.*, p. 60.

If, in order to construct an artistic form, any medium must not only produce meaning, it must also imply a consideration of its own historic conventions at any given moment,[19] in Stan Douglas's work, the relation between present and past is plunged into a complexity of meanings, when one historical moment engages with another. The re-enactment of a time past presupposes a dialectical undertaking that renders that time legible to the eyes of the present. Stan Douglas's work has been discussed several times, and with some pertinence, from a redemptive, Benjaminian perspective. Nevertheless, an artistic form is not simply a mediation undertaken in the present as the labour of interpretation of the past. Rather, artistic form is positioned in a present that is produced out of a past, and from the process of becoming of other artistic forms, bearers of historical conventions and consensuses concerning the mediums that determine and produce not only the significations of that past, but also the potentialities of another present. Thus, it is through the forms of knowledge they produce, and in their historical transience, their practices and dissentions, that mediums are redefined from an explicit perspective, one that is a far cry from simple revisionism. They then take on board an implicit formulation, in its realisations for the present, actualising new possibilities.

19 Thierry de Duve defines the concept of medium thus: "the medium in its specificity is not simply a matter of physical constituents; it comprises technical know-how, cultural habits, working procedures and disciplines — all the conventions of a given art whose definition is throughout historical — even more so that the self-critical (or self-referential, but better called reflexive) tendency of modernism is to take those conventions for subject matter and to test their aesthetic validity. This means that the conventions of a specific art such as painting are never a given. They are the momentary and fragile state of a consensus that is bound to be broken before it is reconstituted elsewhere." Thierry de Duve, *Kant after Duchamp*. Cambridge, Mass. & London: October Books/The MIT Press, 1996, p. 210.

In turn, the discursive practice of history too does not constitute a temporal continuity, always formed out of discontinuous segments. Rather, it unpacks temporal discontinuities through their repeated returns and actualisations, in a process where the construction of utterances corresponds to intelligibilities. In this manner, the discontinuity made manifest by the present state of the medium in relation to images and narratives from the past, renders possible the exercise of construction and the return-as-becoming supported by a recursive structure that is activated. As Susan Buck-Morss explains it, "the presentation of the historical object within a charged force field of past and present, which produces political electricity in a 'lightning flash' of truth, is the 'dialectical image.'"[20]

While there is no medium determinism, since the recursive structure of the medium does not make specific pronouncements about history or any other matter, it is also not possible to conceive a state of fiction without the structure of a medium, incorporating the specific apparatus of resources and conventions that produces it. Implicitly, the production of an artistic form is derived from a confrontation of various considerations of the medium, all demanding intelligibility. Giorgio Agamben, who considers "an apparatus literally everything that has in some way the capacity of capturing, determining, orienting, intercepting, shaping, guiding, securing, or controlling the behaviour, gestures, opinion, discourses of living beings or substances." He suggests that "language itself [is] perhaps the oldest apparatus" considers the subject to be the production of "hand-to-hand combat of a living being and an apparatus."[21] From this, it becomes clear that there is no single process of subjectification or,

20 Susan Buck-Morss, *op. cit.*, p. 219.
21 Giorgio Agamben, *Qu'est-ce qu'un dispositif?* Paris: Éditions Payot & Rivages, 2007, pp. 31-32. Translation mine.

if we so wish, of the production of artistic form, but rather, multiple means for a single individual, and an infinite amount of them for the totality of these processes. This is not to suggest that a medium is neutral to the intentionality of a subject, as certain forms of modernism have hypothesised; nor does it mean that the medium is circumscribed by the distribution of the sensible and the intelligible that an automatism governs, as a certain technological determinism fostering other modernist utopias would have it. It is, then, important to analyse the profound revision to which cinematic models, photo-journalism, and the recording of musical performance on film, have been submitted, as well as the subversion that attends it.

CASE STUDIES

Luanda–Kinshasa is a video projection tracking a band playing in a recording studio. They are playing fusion music, somewhere between jazz, funk, jazz-rock, elec-tronic, and afrobeat, in which tablas contribute to the rhythmical elaboration of the classical music of India. The clothes and the general look of the musicians, who are of different ethnicities, as well as the musical struc-tures, enable one to place the action in the early 1970s. Indeed, these musicians could well have been a part of the line-up performing before or after Miles Davis at the *Cascais Jazz* session on 20 November 1971. As they are in a studio recording session, with headphones and moveable room dividers separating them, the frames are held around each of them, and their concentrated gazes fluctuate between interiority and a visual dialogue suggested by the music, enabling the montage to pass from one shot to the next, from one musician to the next. Thus, it seems that the montage is an integral part of the musical structure. For any specialist in the matter, the studio itself is recognisable as *The Church*, a building on 30ᵗʰ Street, New York, whose previous function was religious, acquired by Columbia Records in 1949, where Miles Davis recorded his albums between 1954 and 1981.

A specific clue to the date on which this recording took place may be directly deduced from the fact that a friend or participant reads a book during the session, the autobiography of Charles Mingus, *Beneath the Underdog*, published precisely in 1971. The filming, and the situation, might at first glance remind a film buff of a section of the film *One Plus One* (1968) by Jean-Luc Godard, where we are party to a studio recording of *Sympathy for the Devil* by the Rolling Stones. Indeed, it is this genre – the documentary – that Stan Douglas rearticulates in *Luanda–Kinshasa*.

In a documentary film like *Luanda–Kinshasa*, a film buff would also recognise the musicians, as is the case in *One Plus One*, where they are fictional characters. The fact is that, although musicians are playing, this is not a soundtrack with an autonomous existence outside of Stan Douglas's film. What we have here are musicians who act to camera, not simulating, yet being fictional characters, since they take on board a fictional situation. This ambiguity underlines the *might have been* of the situation, since the real and the fictional exist simultaneously. The conditional tense of the verb is, furthermore, reinforced by props and costumes that slip back from the present time of the recording, towards the past. If, once again, we invoke a specialist, this time a music buff, this "past" reveals another ambiguity, since the sound is from a particular moment in the history of Afro-American music, and the allusion to Miles Davis is obvious.

In his brilliant analysis of this work, Diedrich Diederichsen observes that "there is also a glaring absence in *Luanda–Kinshasa*. I am speaking, obviously, of Miles himself."[22] The studio was his, and the music evokes a particular period in his work, characterised by the increased fusion with other musical genres, fostering a conversation with that of other, younger musicians in genres such as funk, electronic, jazz-rock, or even Indian music. Stan Douglas himself notes, however, that in 1972, Miles Davis recorded *On the Corner*, which, despite this dialogue with other genres attracting new audiences, was a commercial fiasco. He was not to record in studio again until 1981. In this sense, this "soundtrack" seems to grant continuity to a temporal disjunction in the past.

An attentive musical analysis would invoke yet another experimental context that did not become the object of fusion in the musical utopia that Miles Davis embodied. This was afrobeat, a style of music developed in 1972 by the Cameroonian musician Manu Dibango, with synthesised fusions of jazz and afrofunk, emerging specifically in the album *Soul Makossa*. He was actually criticised, by more orthodox fans, for creating a piece of music that was less African, but he always defended the freedom of musicians to absorb the most diverse of influences as the prerogative on any musician. The fact is that Manu Dibango's afrobeat and Miles Davis's jazz never really crossed paths, except in *Luanda–Kinshasa*, which grants continuity to the utopia that these two musicians undertook as an intercultural dialogue, one made possible by the decolonisation of the African continent.

It is also because of the missed encounter between these two musicians, via their absence, that the musicians return to *The Church*, in order to actualise a possibility.

22   Diedrich Diederichsen, "The eye of the trumpet", *in* León Krempel (ed.), *Stan Douglas. Mise en scène*. Munich: Prestel Verlag, 2014, exhibition catalogue (Haus der Kunst, Munich; Irish Museum of Modern Art, Dublin; and Carré d'Art, Nimes), p. 148.

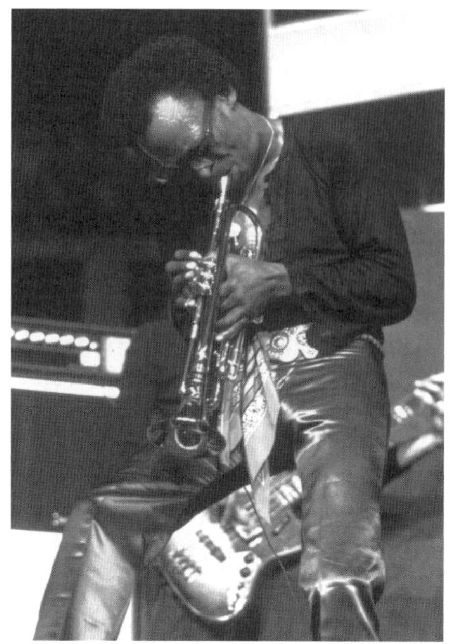

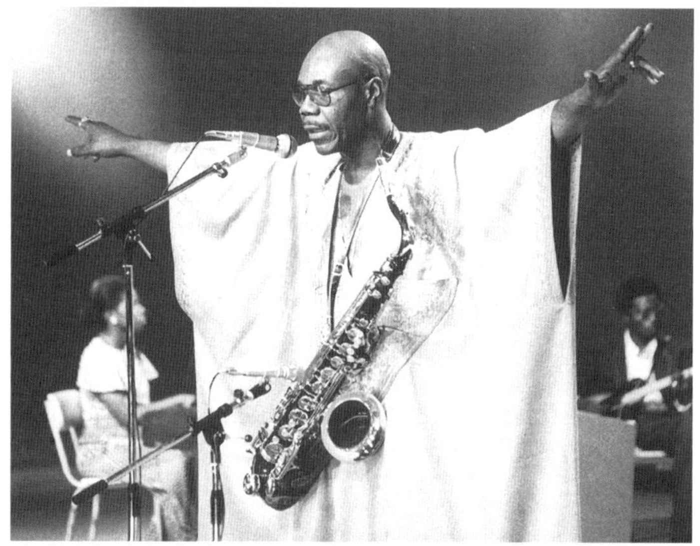

D   Miles Davis at *Cascais Jazz'71*, Cascais International Jazz Festival, 1971.
Photograph by José Carlos Nascimento.
E   Manu Dibango, c. 1972.

This can only take place as the phantasmagoria that the film presents to us. Stan Douglas notes that during Miles Davis' nine-year absence from this recording studio, during which he only made live recordings, Teo Macero of Columbia Records edited, under Davis' supervision, the innumerable recordings that he'd undertaken in the meanwhile, and that through this work of editing, Miles was thus able to "complete the compositional process itself."[23] The musical pieces that we hear in *Luanda–Kinshasa* were created by the montage of the film itself. All of the segments are approximately of the same duration, and each is centred round a musician, whose instrument is at times slightly amplified in relation to the sound of the whole group. The passage to the next section is realised commutatively through random possibilities. The same combination would take six hours to reappear; it is through a random process of recombination that the musical segments and filmed shots generate the musical composition and narrative structure of the film.

If the glances that the musicians exchange express a fluctuation between dialogue and introspection, in the context of a musical typology based on the relations between the freedom of improvisation on the one hand, and previously determined common themes on the other, this process of musical performance incorporates a manifest theatricality. Such theatricality is also a feature of the re-combinations implicit in the mechanism of the film's making, since it is from the cues given in glances that another filmic sequence is launched. This is a performative dimension productive of a network of heterogeneities inhabiting the movement of these bodies, implicit in the indissolubility of image and music assumed by the digital. The indeterminacy of the place of the

23 Stan Douglas's notes.

subjects and of their acts, linked to the evolution of the
music and the filmic narrative, constitutes the above-
mentioned theatricality.[24]

However, there is no longer an opposition between
live and *studio* recording, as Miles Davis seems to have
suggested with his live recordings and his studio editing.
The musical performance now takes place simultaneously
in both places, entailing an oscillation and a meandering,
and as a result, breaks up the unity of each individual
subject, which now returns in these alternations as plural-
ity. Indeed, the easing of a musical structure in favour of
free improvisation and the exploration of individual styles
melded in the fluency of the combo and held together
by a hypnotic beat underpinning Miles Davies' musical
project from 1965 onward, pointed towards the impossibility of restoring any kind of unity. What returns,
in the motion produced by the sum of film sequences,
are the spectres of each body, indistinguishable from
a performance produced through digital process. It is
in this sense that *Luanda–Kinshasa* arouses and grants
continuity to a bifurcation that is waiting to happen,
in a time now lost, reaching us as the spectrality that
inhabits an automatism, granting us a future past.

The fact is that if, on the one hand, theatricality
produces the musicians' performance and that of the film,
on the other hand, it is in excess of the system in which it
originates — a system that determines the temporal order
to which each sequence has been previously primed by
the recursive structure of the apparatus and plays with

24 Here, I am following the notion of theatricality as defined by Samuel
Weber, not to confused with theatre as an institutional system. For Weber,
"this irreducible opacity defines the quality of theatre as *medium*. When
an event or series of events *takes place* without reducing the place it 'taken'
to a purely neutral site, then that place reveals itself to be a 'stage,' and those
events become theatrical happenings. [...] [S]uch happenings never take
place once and for all but are ongoing" *in* Samuel Weber, *Theatricality as
Medium*. New York: Fordham University Press, 2004, p. 7.

randomness. Between a theatricality-as-event and an apparatus as structure, a new subjectification of the past becomes possible. That its condition is spectral is inevitable, by virtue of representing a utopian culmination of a multicultural dialogue. It is also our globalised present of unilateral "conversations" that its spectrality haunts.

In Cascais in 1971, faced with Charlie Haden and the Ornette Coleman Quartet's dedication of their set to the liberation movements and the raised fists of musicians and public alike, the impotence of the police was an obvious sign that somewhere, a line was being drawn. A new phase dawned with the revolution of 25 April 1974. This brought to a close one of the oldest dictatorships in Europe, and an unsustainable colonial war, contested by the broad sectors of Portuguese society. At a time when revolution in Europe was no longer expected, well after May '68, it in fact occurred in a country that was manifestly out of step with the times in the rest of the West. The revolution, consummated by a group of captains organised within the Armed Forces Movement (MFA) that was supported by the population at large, took place almost peacefully. The vast wave of popular support, dubbed "Aliança Povo-MFA" (People's Alliance with MFA), generated a wave of incommensurable joy and a revolutionary dynamic, rapidly gathering momentum but also making manifest the existence of differing views, and tensions concerning the revolutionary process itself. This alliance constituted one of the most significant aspects of a direct democracy, with the MFA overcoming governmental paralysis and bureaucracy, together with the popular movements that sprang out of the profound problems that cut across the whole of Portuguese society. The alliance was born of direct action, becoming — in the popular imagination — a symbol of the loosening of social problems. The situation in international politics, stabilised

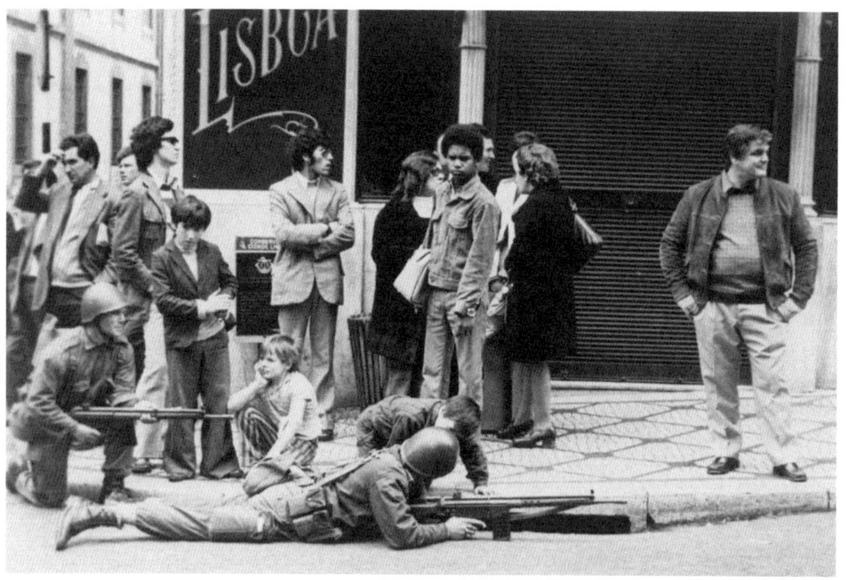

F

F   MFA (Armed Forces Movement) troops seal off access to Largo do Carmo, Lisbon, 25 April 1974. Photograph by Alfredo Cunha.

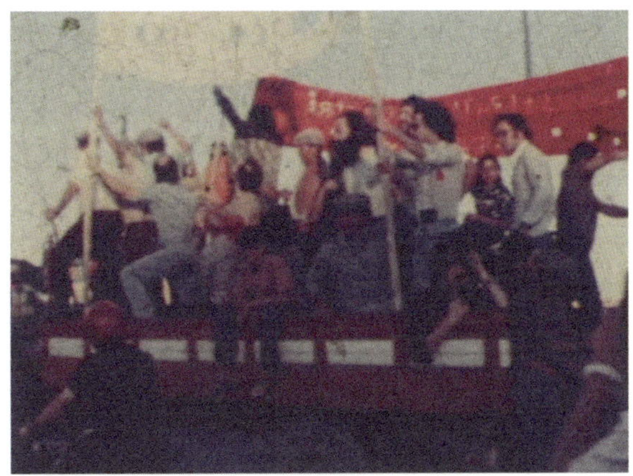

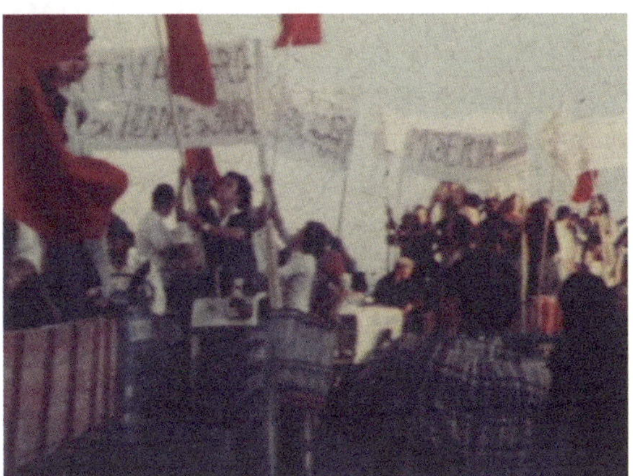

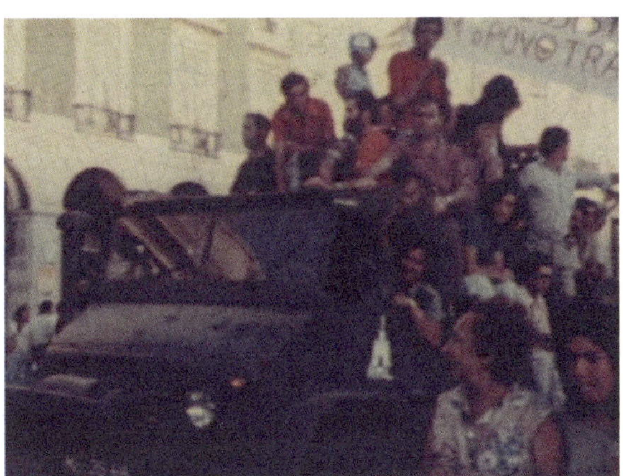

G

G   Demonstration in support of the "COPCON document" in Lisbon on
20 August 1975, with the participation of workers from Lisbon's industrial belt
and shipyards, rural workers, soldiers and sailors. Images filmed in Super 8 by
Ernesto de Sousa.

in the context of the Cold War and the politics of the blocs, did not prove to be favourable to the aspirations of the Left, because Portugal is part of the North Atlantic Treaty Organisation (NATO), and under the sway of the USA.

In March 1975, the *New York Times* proclaimed that NATO had imposed "a kind of quarantine" on Portugal, and the United States Secretary of Defence, James Schlesinger, advocated the necessity of an action that "will have to take some symbolic form – making them outcasts without casting them out." Henry Kissinger, United States Secretary of State proclaimed that the leftward turn in Portugal "will of course raise question for the United States in relationship to its NATO policy and to its policy toward Portugal," confessing that the Washington was "disquieted by an evolution in which there is a danger that the democratic process may become a sham."[25] Suspicions grew around the possibility that the Ambassador of the USA in Portugal, Frank Carlucci, and the Central Intelligence Agency (CIA) itself had been involved in the attempted coup of 11 March, although the Ambassador issued a public denial of any such involvement.

The Secret Agent is an adaptation of the celebrated, eponymous novella by Joseph Conrad, published in 1907, its conversion into a cinematic installation consisting of six screens arranged in two equal sets on opposite walls of a large, darkened space. The memory of one of the earliest instances of multiple screen installations, namely *Glimpses of the USA* (1959) by Charles and Ray Eames, constitutes a significant point of reference for this work. This is a feature-length film with a chronological narrative plot. However, this filmic genre

25   David Binder, "U.S., in Message to Lisbon, Says Move Left is a Danger to NATO," *The New York Times*, 27 March, 1975, p. 2.

undergoes profound changes, beginning with the way the installation is set up, enabling the presentation of each scene to be distributed among two or three screens, thus immersing the observer in a way that is different from single-screen cinema.

In Joseph Conrad's novella, Verloc, an anarchist with secret links to an embassy, is charged with bombing the Greenwich Observatory, greatest icon of scientific knowledge. Stan Douglas's installation displaces the action to the context of Portugal in the period of PREC (Revolutionary Process Underway) following 25 April 1974. The characters bear the names of those in the book, but they are updated to suit the context. Verloc is now the son of a good English family, born in Oporto. After participating in the upheaval wreaked by anarchist groups in Paris in May '68, and having been arrested for acts of sedition, he returns to Portugal, where he runs a small cinema, enabling him to hold meetings with other anarchists and disguise his secret activities. At the cinema, he also sells both revolutionary and surrealist literature, recently published with the lifting of the censorship laws. A poster at the cinema enables us to identify the film currently on show as *Last Tango in Paris*.[26] Verloc's wife wife Winnie has a son named Stevie from an earlier marriage, and not being completely informed about the activities of Verloc and his friends, such as Ossipon, Michaelis and Karl Yundt, she fearfully intuits what is happening. Things move quickly on and her deduction then occupies the hiatus between the dramatic events that we have already suspected.

The first scene is at dawn, at the US Embassy,

26 Bernardo Bertolucci's film was a great success when it came out in 1972, but owing to censorship laws in Portugal, it was banned. After the revolution, the film was able to be viewed, and enjoyed great success. There were even organised excursions from Spain to Lisbon for the viewing of the film, because Spain was then still in the stranglehold of Franco's dictatorship, which also banned the film. In this conversation, Yundt makes an allusion to the queues waiting to see this film.

where a secret meeting takes place between Verloc and
Vladimir, First Secretary, who demands efficient action.
Bearing in mind the imminent elections, he states:
"we don't want prevention we a want cure [...] Portugal
must be brought into line."[27] After analysing the social
situation, he concludes that the only thing that interests
the Portuguese is the future, so that it is modernity itself
that needs to be exploded. Following upon the isola-
tionism that fascism had fostered, communication
networks with the world become the proposed target.
To blow up the Marconi installation in Sesimbra, linking
European communication networks to the American
continent, is the objective defined by Vladimir in order to
restrain the middle class at the time of voting. The scene
is initially distributed among three screens. The use of this
structure determines the complex mode of presentation
that the rest of the film sustains in relation to the observer.

Employing a similar structure, the following scenes
frame the topologies of the extreme Left and of anarchism,
and the scene bringing together Ossipon, a French
Maoist, with the Professor, an anarchist individualist
and also a bomber, close to Max Stirner, is an example
of this. The Professor is permanently booby-trapped so
that, in the event of detention, he can blow himself up.
His defence of violence situates him beyond mere instru-
mentality, at the service of a cause, so that he takes on
a sacrificial role, dissociated from an aim outside of his
own means, as an exercise of sovereignty as an exception
to collective life. In a later scene, he states: "I stand apart
from everything artificial. They depend upon the social
order, which [...] is complex and open to attack. I, on the
other hand, depend on death, which is simple and cannot
be attacked. My superiority is self-evident."[28]

27 Stan Douglas, screenplay, *The Secret Agent*, 2015 (in this book, p. 146).
28 *Loc. cit*, p. 164.

In another scene, we're shown Verloc with his political cell at the cinema. In their constrained dialogues, they talk in the name of a historical subject, the proletariat, and of its direction, or even manipulation, alongside cynical opportunism. Ossipon justifies the ambiguous strategy whereby he lives with regard to the MFA, by quoting R.D. Laing: "They are playing a game. They are playing at not playing a game. If I show them I see they are, I shall break the rules and they will punish me. I must play their game, of not seeing I see the game."[29] It is, then, between a transcendent violence, intended to be sacrificial, supported by the Professor's individualist anarchism, and Ossipon and Michaelis's cynical class position, disguised as Maoism, that a topology is outlined, determining the forces that shake this community gathered around Verloc. Through a new encounter between the Professor and Ossipon, we are given to understand that the attack, whose order is given by the First Secretary, has taken place, despite the fact that the Marconi mission failed to meet its objective and despite the fact that there had already been one unforeseen victim.

From the Professor, we understand that Verloc has ordered the bomb. The tension of the situation is not confined to the film dialogue, but is conveyed by the music as well, performed on one of the other screens by a guitarist playing autonomous variations on the theme "Clear Spot" by Captain Beefheart and The Magic Band, and a keyboard player. This seems to propel the unfolding of the situations and makes way for the full expression of the rhetorical elements of the cinematographic apparatus. Added to this is the fact that these musical variations are not coincident with the same scenes upon each viewing.

The acknowledgement of the attack by the police and political powers takes place through a dialogue

29 *Loc. cit*, p. 154.

between Chief Inspector Heat, a diligent and politically indifferent policeman, and the assistant commissioner, a veteran of the colonial war, at the service of COPCON.[30] It is understood that Heat and Verloc not only know each other, but that they had also exchanged confidences. Heat knew of Verloc's links to the US Embassy, and thanks to intelligence provided by Verloc, was able to have a career that earned him recognition. Heat tells him that in the remains of an unrecognisable corpse, on which Verloc's address had been found. The Chief Inspector then visits Winnie and questions her, telling her what happened. When he shows Winnie a photograph of the boot found near the remains of the body, Winnie realises that the corpse must be that of her son, who'd been on holiday near Sesimbra, at Michaelis' house.

In the meanwhile, Verloc appears and Heat questions him, convinced that he was the second man involved in the attack, the one who had managed to get away unharmed. On another screen, we see the public watching a film, ignorant of the vicissitudes happening alongside them. Nevertheless, as this is incorporated into the show-ing of the same scene, it seems suddenly that this public is enlisted to view the climax of the narrative. We're shown another, unrelated film, but since it is incorporated into that scene, it seems to be suddenly enlisted as part of the climax of the narrative. When Chief Inspector Heat leaves, Verloc tries to explain to Winnie, who had heard the conversation, about the accident. She is beside herself. She pushes him against a shelf bracket, which enters the base of his spine, killing him. Then Ossipon appears, to confirm that what he's read in the papers is true. Despairing, Winnie tries to escape with him,

30 Comando Operacional do Continente (Continental Operational Commando), the political police created by the MFA after the revolution to ensure the application of a system of justice that had been missing from the earlier institutions that had taken on board the same function during the fascist regime.

but when he goes out, to supposedly buy train tickets, he drops the money Winnie had given him and is caught by a policeman, who is suspicious that he had robbed the cinema. He is made to return there. When the officer sees Verloc's body Ossipon denounces Winnie. After Heat's arrival, we see her taken to the police station in a long shot that occupies one whole screen, the Chief Inspector, at the entrance to the cinema, finds the Professor, whom he asks if he's proud of himself. At this very moment, the Professor realises that Verloc was not the victim of the failed attack, but of a murder, the circumstances of which it is not in his interest to understand.

The film ends with the Chief Inspector giving instructions to the police, not to "let the crowd contaminate the scene!" Turning to the Professor, Chief Inspector Heat says: "Maybe a crowd will one day tear you to pieces." To which the other murmurs: "Ah yes. The crowd. Filthy countless multitude. Unconscious. Blind... Let them."[31] It is in this revulsion expressed by the Professor, in his attempt to salvage a sovereign legitimacy founded on the exception of a subject in opposition to the common, that the anarchist individualism of the Professor, and by extension, the cynicism of the other leftists is manifested against the indeterminacy of common life, the potential to be affirmative, that confers upon the subject a decisive sovereignty or constitutive,[32] as Stan Douglas seems to suggest with his reference to "multitude.") They all agree with the Chief Inspector when he insists that the multitude not contaminate the scene. The indeterminacy of common life or of the multitude that presupposes its sovereign power or its

31   Stan Douglas, *op. cit*, p. 202.
32   Antoni Negri, *Insurgencies: Constituent Power and the Modern State*. Minneapolis: University of Minnesota Press, 1999, pp. 21-22. For Negri, constituent power is an act of choice over that which does not yet exist, "[...] whose conditions of existence imply that the creative act does not lose its characteristics in the act of creating."

constituting power is never determined by the existing order, neither is it proposed by the more or less opportunistic revolutionary manuals, but rather, appear as a free potentiality and praxis.[33]

The sacrifice of an innocent, Winnie's son Stevie, configures the erasure until exclusion of the difference between the freedom of the young man's life and its destruction, whether voluntary or involuntary – for the purposes of this argument, there is no difference – through action and political conformity. In involving Stevie in terrorist activity, Verloc, ruled by the mechanism of a modern democratic potency, reproduces the aims of the latter, to transform natural life into a form of political life, submitting it to its suspension as bare life,[34] and to the supreme violence of its suppression, a process that Giorgio Agamben finds in modern democracies, identifying its end as "an inner solidarity between democracy and totalitarianism."[35] It is not a matter of erasing the differences between democracy and totalitarian states, neither is it about obfuscating personal histories, but rather, of understanding, in this convergence, the sustained submission of natural life to political form, whether it be

33   For Giorgio Agamben "[t]he problem of constituting power then becomes the problem of the 'constitution of potentiality' (*Il potere costituente*, p. 383) and the unresolved dialectic between constituting power and constituted power opens the way for a new articulation of the relation between potentiality and actuality, which requires nothing less than a rethinking of the ontological categories of modality in their totality. [...] Only an entire new conjunction of possibility and reality, contingency and necessity [...] will make it possible to cut the knot that binds sovereignty to constituting power." Giorgio Agamben, *Homo Sacer: Sovereign Power and Bare Life*, transl. Daniel Heller-Roazen. Stanford, California: Stanford University Press, 1998, no. 17, p. 44. To the extent that potentiality is owns its non-power and thus safeguards this lack of distinction, it is sovereign and not determined or preceded by anything.

34   Agamben defines bare life according to the Greek distinction between *zoë* "which expressed the simple fact of living common to all living beings (animals, men, or gods" and *bios* "which indicated the form or way of living proper to an individual or a group," Abamben, *op. cit.*, pp. 9-11.

35   *Op. cit.*, p. 10.

through libertarian claims or through authoritarian vigilance. Stevie's inclusion in an extreme act perpetrated by the alliance Verloc-Vladimir, configures the biopolitical bond constituted by diverse forms of political sovereignty as they seek to appropriate the course of a revolutionary process of liberation. It is the action of the biopolitical bond that leaves him suspended between his natural trajectory and subjection to a political form, and thus to sovereign violence.

It is important to underline that none of these characters is a symbol capable of encapsulating the representation of the principles of a historical situation. They function, rather, as fictional examples, standing alongside that which they exemplify. They share a state of belonging with other historically recorded cases. They merely put into operation the passage from specific situation to general, and vice versa, and may thus be defined as pure discourse. In this context, it is important to clarify the political outcomes of this in the relation between narrative and viewer, effected by the cinematic installation. It is a question of proceeding with a re-articulation of language itself, of a critical and extreme possibility of the medium splitting itself into component parts and questioning the taking-place of its language, and as such, getting to know its own parameters.

We have seen how the use of several screens for the viewing of each scene served to distribute multiple perceptions. In this way, the observer is confronted with a situation that does not keep him at the same safe distance as does the regular cinema seat. On the one hand, if the possibility afforded the observer, of thus acquiring panoptical knowledge of the situation – of viewing a scene and simultaneously seeing what the characters within it cannot see – suggests a power greater than that granted the observer in the traditional specular relationship with the cinema screen, on the other hand, the breaking up

of views into multiple perspectives and the intervals
that these imply, requiring the observer as a source of
coherence through the movements of his own body,
produces a constant sense of loss. This produces the
sensation that something is taking place on the other side
of the installation that I, as the viewing subject, do not see.
In turning around, I've perhaps missed some detail,
perhaps something crucial for the unfolding of the narrative. As one screen lights up, I am forced to turn around.
In addition to this, each new scene is divided among
various screens, none of which is coincidental with the
previous one, and the development of the narrative,
which is temporal, seems to occur in space too, obliging
me to move forwards and backwards in response to its
progression. From being in possession of an ostensible
perceptual control of the film, I become an agent who
actualises, through the contingencies of my movements,
the possibility of the film's very realisation. Indeed, every
scene in the film implies such splitting and unfolding.

While the use of multiple screens for the purposes of
narrative constructions seems to hark back to the notion
of expanded cinema, its sources are in fact earlier than
that. In 1959, at the invitation of George Nelson, designer
of the American National Exhibition in Moscow, Charles
and Ray Eames made a film called *Glimpses of the USA*
that constitutes a significant point of reference for
Douglas's *The Secret Agent*. The Eames film consisted
of a projection synchronised for seven screens measuring
9 × 6 metres each, suspended from a geodesic dome 76
metres in diameter, designed by Buckminster Fuller.
The film presented, in nine minutes, a typical North
American work day, and in three a typical weekend.
It was made up of thousands of still and moving images,
gathered from photographic and film archives by authors
both famous and anonymous, as well as by the Eameses
themselves. The film was narrated with some humour.

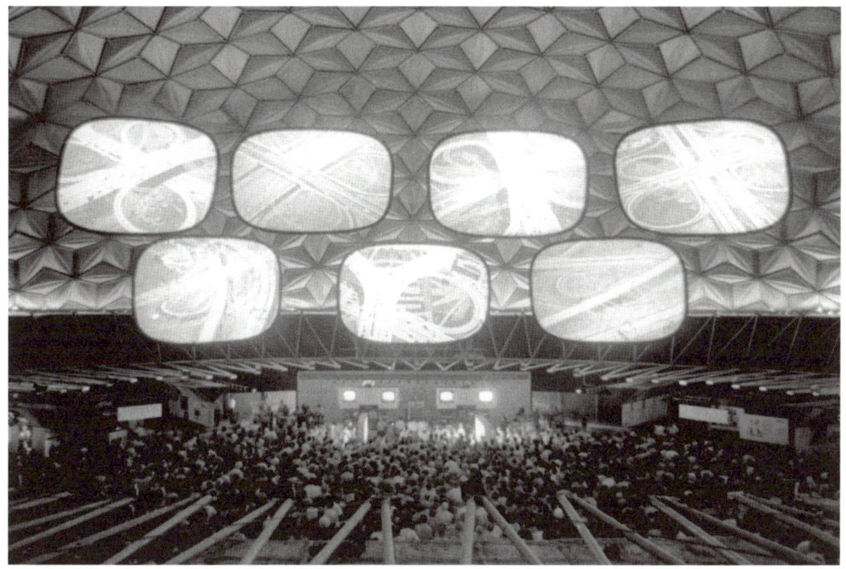

H

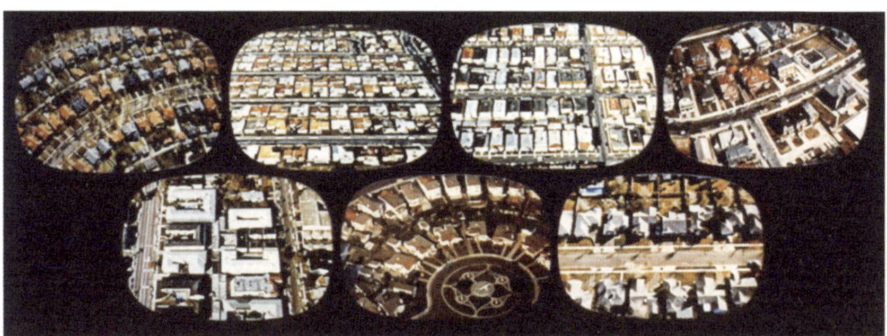

I

H View from inside the geodesic dome designed by Buckminster Fuller with the screens where *Glimpses of the USA* by Charles and Ray Eames was projected in the *American National Exhibition*, Moscow, 1959.
I Charles and Ray Eames, *Glimpses of the USA* (1959). Graphic representation based on photograms of films projected onto seven 9 × 6 screens at the American National Exhibition, Moscow, 1959.

It began with images of the cosmos and of ordinary life both in the USA and in the Soviet Union, in order to demonstrate and underline the differences implicit in North American life, through the use of multiple close-ups subordinated to distinct themes, such as going out to work, cars, the big city, and even the goodnight kiss. The perspectives offered by the seven screens were innovative, emerging from new imaging technologies, such as the telescope, the zoom lens, aerial or night views. This representation of the USA constituted an operation of seduction, minutely masterminded, in order to convince the Soviet public of the advantages of capitalism. In the middle of the Cold War, competition for supremacy in scientific progress was manifest, and if the USA was able to display a bazaar of everyday technologies, as Beatrice Colomina suggests,[36] the Russian newspaper *Izvestia* promptly addressed the dearth of American science, industry and industrial technologies. The launch of *Sputnik* in 1957 constituted that which was latently repressed in this operation, that the purportedly new perception in *Glimpses of the USA* offered. As Colomina suggests, "if *Glimpses* simulates the operation of satellite surveillance, it exposes more than the details of life in the streets: it penetrates the most intimate spaces and reveals every secret."[37]

Following Colomina's thesis, "the technological model for multiscreen, multimedia presentations may have been provided by the war situation room, which was designed in those same years to bring information in simultaneously from numerous sources around the world so that the president and the military comanders

36 Beatriz Colomina, "Enclosed by images: the Eamese's multiscreen architecture», *Grey Room* 02 (Winter 2001), Cambridge, Mass.: MIT Press Journals. This essay was republished in Stan Douglas and Christopher Eamon (eds.), *Art of Projection*. Ostfildern: Hatje Cantz Verlag, 2009, revealing its relevance for Stan Douglas.
37 *Ibid.*, p. 13.

could make critical decisions."[38] Indeed, friends of the Eameses were involved in the conception of such projects, reinforcing an argument in favour of a proximity and common genealogy between various types of multimedia presentation, such as *Glimpses of the USA,* with panoptical systems of control. Nevertheless, the informational complexity of such multimedia events, at least in this example by the Eameses, leaves this a moot question. On the one hand, in the vertigo of multiple images, we see clearly the imperative to transmit, in the twelve-minute duration of the film, the largest possible quantity of information: in this sense, the film breaks with traditional narrative models, substituting them with a new conceptualisation of information that reveal themselves in continuous cuts and collages of a gigantic archive, anticipating the era of the computer in its relationship with memory and with history itself. On the other hand, in over-reaching the limit that would enable any observer to be conscious of the number of images given within each instant, the seven screens produce an informational overload that emphasises a dispersive attention, digressing in the accumulation of fragments. In this way, what was shown was not the manner in which a previously constituted subject might perceive objectivity from the outside world, but rather, how this subject came to be constructed through informational systems. If control centres of wars are present in this multiple screen device, their reconfiguration as propaganda, carried out by the Eameses, exposes something else: that distractive perception has become predominant in subjectivity, manifestly as it has in the process of modernity.

In an essay titled "On the aesthetics of video installations," Boris Groys concludes (and not only with

38 *Ibid.,* p. 15.

regard to the work of Stan Douglas) that "the additional aesthetic value of a museum-based video installation lies above all in explicitly raising the issue of the lack of overall view, certainty and control on the part of the viewer."[39] It is in this sense that the fragmentation to which the film is submitted through the autonomy of its components "liberates the film image as such from a certain zone of inarticulacy and opens it up to film-theoretical discourse." This configuration, taken on by the cinematic installation, enables the viewer to constitute an acute reflexivity for each element, as well as sponsoring a sense of unfamiliarity with regard to the traditional modes of cinematic presentation.

The multiplication of each scene onto several screens and the spatial relations thus established perform a profound revision in the relations of the film to fictional space, the physicality of its presentation, and the sensoriality of the observer. As Juliane Rebentisch has noted: "so the viewer — like the viewer of Minimalist arrangements — will experience cinematographic installation in an important sense as *his* situation […] in the installation at any given moment."[40] At root, it forces the observer out of the traditional immersion of cinema, sponsoring a crisis in what Jacques Lacan described as "that in which the consciousness may turn back upon itself,"[41] in other words the function that enables the subject to see in each representation a reflection of himself, as the intentional dominion of observation itself, in an imaginary relation that produces the spectator as consciousness of the image.

39   Boris Groys, "On the aesthetics of video installations" *in* Peter Pakesch (ed.), *Stan Douglas. Le Détroit*, Basel: Kunsthalle Basell; Schwabe, 2001, exhibition catalogue, no pagination.
40   Juliane Rebentisch, *Aesthetics of Installation Art*. Berlin: Stenberg Press, 2012, p. 182.
41   Jacques Lacan, "The eye and the gaze," in *The Four Fundamental Concepts of Psycho-Anhalysis*, transl. Alan Sheridan. London: Penguin Books, 1987, p. 75.

Linking the role of the imaginary to the constitution of the subject, and this subject's way of experiencing social relations, with the concept of the cinematic apparatus — the economic, the technical and the ideological components that constitute a medium — film theorists such as Christian Metz, Jean-Louis Baudry, Stephen Heath and Laura Mulvey, among others defined the representations produced by the institution of cinema and presented on the screen as the direct assumption of the consciousness of the subject through relations of identification offered by the imaginary. In film theory, the effect of a literal impression of reality replaced the old relation of verisimilitude between image and its referent in the real by the fit between subject and image, assumed as the specific representation of the subject and its world.

Now in *The Secret Agent*, the images installed in real space foster the intrusion of physical space into narrative time, and into fictional time in the viewing space. Thanks to the mutual intrusion of time and space, the installation does not present a fully defined, constituted entity; its presence is, rather, suspended in the interval between what is presented and the presentation itself. Its present time then comes to be defined through the convergence of its articulation with that which is articulated. *The Secret Agent* thus renders conscious the physical experience of the gaze.[42]

The sound track, too, is variously distributed through the scenes of the film in their various repetitions, so that that the traditional association of musical sequence

42 Stan Douglas's position with regard to this question is enlightening: As an artist, I've taken to identifying my film works as "sculpture" to certain museums, just to avoid them deciding to transfer my films to DVD and projecting on some crappy LCD projector." Stan Douglas and Christopher Eamon, "Regarding shadows," in *Beyond Cinema: The Art of Projection: Films, Videos and Installations from 1963 to 2005*. Ostfildern: Hatje Cantz Verlag, 2006, exhibition catalogue (Hamburger Bahnhof — Museum für Gegenwart, Berlin), p. 17.

with narrative is different at each viewing, construing at the root of one's memory an unpredictable return of the diegetic scene, giving rise to the unfolding of difference with each repetition. The perception of the film thus springs from an exchange between the body, the visible and the audible, as well as the reversibility of the latter terms. For Merleau-Ponty,[43] this mutual intrusion of body and perception produces something invisible, a kind of interval between the perceived world and the perceiving gaze. The interposition of this interval not only strips the subject of a perception of the rational structures that confirm this subject as a self that is projected in the consciousness of the film, but also produces that very self as a spectre upon the scene of the revolution. We thus find ourselves before the theatricality of the cinematographic apparatus, implicit in a structure that critiques the violence of forms of political sovereignty advanced in the plot. Simultaneous to the observer's gaze fluctuating continuously between various perceptions, it is stripped of its power to appropriate the whole and to press upon it the representation of the subject's world, so akin to the teleological or biopolitical perspectives, or the constituted powers to which the characters in the film wish to submit the world.

It is, then a double negation of the historical substrates of the device of multiple screens that Stan Douglas realises with *The Secret Agent*: on the one hand, through the integration of its wish for a historical panopticism in the relationship of the characters with the revolution, even if, in their capacity as characters, they are always submitted to the general determinations of a narrative that they cannot control, just as they can't control the revolution; on the other hand, in placing,

43 Maurice Merleau-Ponty, "Eye and Mind" in *The Primacy of Perception*. James E. Edie (ed.). Trans. Carleton Dallery. Evanston, IL: Northwestern UP, 1964, pp. 159-190.

in the position of control, a spectator produced ay a distractive perception, one that occurred historically with the generalised use of this device for the dispersal of non-differentiated information, and which, as such, does not reproduced any teleological projection on the course of the narrative, subtracting himself from the wishes uttered by the characters. In this exchange of positions and relations, producing a double negation on the previous configurations of the medium, we are given a glimpse of another politics of means. Here, the spectator's position is constructed in the singularities of an experience. These singularities have, as their aim, the power of life itself as the form of life of a multitude, or of any being, given to thought at a historic interval that, for a few instants, seems to suspend the workings of the biopolitical machine. Revolutionary cinema as a means of thinking the revolution.

Disco Angola consists of a series of eight photographs that bring together two distinct realities: the Portuguese decolonisation of Angola in 1974-5 and the start of the civil war on the one hand, and on the other hand, the emergence, at around the same time, of disco sound in the underground clubs of New York, such as the club *Le Jardin*. What links these two series is the same fictional authorship by a photo-journalist whose interest is piqued by the emergence of a new musical form and the culture that surrounds it, producing a series of photographs in 1974 and 1975 (and hence, the inclusion of the dates in the titles of the photographs) of clubs where disco sound gathered a heterogeneous public, composed of various cultures and communities. Afro-Americans, Latino-Americans, Italo-Americans, Wasps, psychedelics, gays and those without specific identity tags all came together in clubs to dance to the strains of a musical form born of fusion, linking funk, soul, pop, salsa, psychedelic and electronic, as an alternative to the rock music that then occupied centre stage of the musical scene for the young.

Once again, Manu Dibango's work *Soul Makossa* (1972) plays a significant role, demonstrating how the importation of current musical productions from other continents exercised an equally decisive influence on this musical form. The reestablishment of music's close links with the body, mediated by dance to hypnotic electronic rhythms onto which simple melodic, harmonic and sensual structures were superimposed, redefined this new relationship, bringing dance back as the privileged reception of music, a role that was underplayed in rock music. In *Club Versailles, 1974*, a high angle shot shows us a dance floor where cultural diversity, as it shapes small group, creates a common space through dance. More than a simple cloakroom, *Coat Check, 1974*, presents us with a large sofa flanked by powerful speakers and various clothes strewn around it, suggesting that the multicultural revolution has extended to meet the sexual revolution that had begun a few years earlier. And perhaps it is precisely this aspect that produces the climax of this multicultural utopia. In *Two Friends, 1975*, we see a couple, dressed in the sophisticated fashion of the day; but this is not a traditional couple. Rather, these are two friends with similar aims having fun at a party, but the scenes are concurrent, rather than allowing the two characters to engage with one another. What we have here is an archaeology of types of behaviour relating to a proliferation of sexual orientations. *Kung Fu Fighting, 1975*, alludes directly to the eponymous song by Carl Douglas and Biddu, that reached no. 1 in the sales charts of 1974 the world over. Indeed, the culture industry rapidly assimilated disco sound and finally, its fragile multicultural utopia became yet another commercial form, but it did bring about the emergence of new publics, new geographies and new cultures.

The second series of photographs that incorporates Angola in 1974-1975 was made, according to the dating, alongside the first, though dealing with different realities. It is, perhaps, the very limits established by these differences between them that we need to understand. We might presume that the fictitious author of these photographic works moved between Angola and New York during this period; but that beyond professional contingency, there remains a doubt as to the reasons for merging these two series. *A Luta Continua, 1974* signals and celebrates, in particular for those who were photographed, the arrival in Luanda of the MPLA, as a consequence of the revolution in Portugal of 25 April 1974, adjuring the end of the colonial war. This initiated the talks that led to the independence of Angola. The existence of three movements of national liberation, three organised and mutually antagonistic parties — the MPLA, the FNLA and UNITA — explains the war-cry "a luta continua e a vitória é certa" (the struggle continues and victory is certain) from which emerges the hint of a complex solution concerning future power.

Capoeira, 1974 gives us, in a high angle shot, a scene depicting the martial art of capoeira that originated in Angola. *Capoeira* was initially a form of combat between slaves, with movements close to the ground, but also including lifting the feet above the head, as is the case in the photograph. This practice was later stylised as dance, accompanied by music with a rhythmic beat, slow and elemental. When practiced in small, bushy enclaves, which then became designated as *capoeiras*, this combat was a mortal struggle; when practiced on the plantations, it assumed a more inoffensive character, and was thence transformed into a dance, enabling it to survive as a symbol of the resistance struggle against the capture that doomed subjects to slavery. As all other instruments are lacking, applause might serve, as it does here when a group of soldiers claps hands, as a symbol according this struggle its place somewhere between ritual and the awakening of a new era.

Exodus, 1975 presents us, in bird's eye view, the rushed departure of the Portuguese colonists and of some of the locals who had family in Portugal, faced with imminent Civil War. In January 1975, the three parties signed the Alvor Agreement in Portugal, with its aim to confirm, ensure and define the transition to independence, aiming for the sharing of power between them, until the first elections and the establishment of independence. The agreement was never fulfilled owing to pressures and external interferences from the USA, South Africa and Zaire supporting FNLA; the Soviet Union and Cuba supporting MPLA; and UNITA initially supported by China, but then also backed by South Africa and the USA, weakening the FNLA. Rapidly, the conflict between the parties spread and from May 1975, more than 15,000 Portuguese registered in Angola sought to return to Portugal, after having been incentivised to move to Africa from the 1940s on by António Salazar. *Checkpoint, 1975,* is a photograph of an area of southern Angola, in the Namib Desert, which was then dominated by UNITA. The presence of a soldier, possibly South African, on the left of the photograph, next to a baobab tree, as well as of two other people and a local child, determines the new division of space and new forms of conflict.

The fact is that, although we may be invited to regard these photographs as eyewitness reports, viewed together, they are perhaps too exemplary in the metonymic way that they render explicit and complex the problems they address. On the other hand, they are not contained by the classic Barthesian trope of photography,

the testimonial "that once was" (*ça a été*), that considers
photographic images to be the indexical traces of a
time past, and hence the need to include the date in the
title of each of the photographs. The re-enactment and
digital manipulation that contributed to the fabrication
of these works seems to call attention to the enigma
of each situation. Some of these photographs allude to
other works of photojournalism from the same period.
But despite the meticulous period reconstruction, incorporating props, landscapes and even styles of framing,
these images invoke a gaze that is temporally external
to the past situation they picture, fostering a return as
memorial consideration. Not only is their scale different
from that of works during the period in question, but
also, their classification as "art" demands relativisation,
since in the period in question, they would certainly
be considered simply as instances of photojournalism.
Documentary photography and historical narrative
as practices of photographic realism, then, are significant aspects of this return realised by re-enactment.
After all, in order to be considered an artistic medium
in its own right, the discursive forms of photography
needed to take on board, in the modern epoch, prior
to the fictional dates of these photographs, the themes
of painting. This occurred precisely on condition that
photography abandon its testimonial role.[44] The re-enactment to which the signs have been submitted in *Disco
Angola* does not permit that mystification that makes a
claim for the possibility of an originary truth to which the
image refers. Such a claim was attendant on some of the
developments in realism. This explains the exclusion of

44 For a profound consideration on the exclusion of discursive practices
from realistic photography, see Benjamin Buchloh "Allan Sekula:
Photography between discourse and document" *in* Allan Sekula, *Fish Story*.
Düsseldorf: Richter Verlag, 1995, exhibition catalogue (Witte de With,
Rotterdam; Fotografiska Museet at the Moderna Museet, Stockholm;
Tramway, Glasgow; and Le Channel, Calais), pp. 189-200.

such claims by a modernity that aimed for the autonomy of the sign. As we saw in the first section of this essay, the documentary foundation constituting an utterance (if we might thus consider these photographs) does not stem from its empirical contents, but rather from a horizon of intelligibility that once granted photographs their conditions of possibility. The event that realist photography celebrates might thus be associated with a historic context in such a way as to produce a discourse capable of engaging a space that is complementary of other, non-discursive practices, for instance economic processes. Bearing in mind a political order for each sign, re-enactment grants these photographs a sense of realism that dissociates itself from traditional models and challenges its historical exclusion by modernism.

Another important feature of *Disco Angola* is linked to a reconsideration of the process of presentation in series. The idea of the photographic series presupposes a model of rapid snapping whose form of organisation and distribution becomes an archive of linked instants in the service of documenting a subject. The photographic image in this context is in a contingent relation with the real and its accumulation produces information in a dynamic way. The related practice is in opposition to photomontage, which stems from collage, and which privileges discontinuity and interval, associating one form with another and thus constructing a relation that is of a semantic order in the interval that articulates one form with another. Thus erupts a visual shock between distinct and fragmented realities. This was the form of composition favoured by modernism, in particular from the Dadaist practices onward, while in turn, the series, emerging from the factographic phase of pro-ductivism, tended toward the register of narration and communication. Stan Douglas's use of re-enactment sets in motion both processes, simultaneously bringing together montage and series, enabling — through continuity and interval — the construction of a discourse on the relationship between the two contexts. At the point where African colonialism ends and a tenuous multi-culturalism emerges in the USA, both are affected by the floundering of a new political and economic world order, bringing war back into the fold, now between global powers and the commercialisation of a product for much broader audiences.

PLAY AND MEMORY

Jonathan Crary has observed that the concept of 24/7 (the book's subtitle is *Late Capitalism and The Ends of Sleep,*) "announces a time without time, a time extracted from any material or identifiable demarca-tions, a time without sequence or recurrence. In its peremptory reductiveness, it celebrates a hallucination of presence, of an unalterable permanence composed of incessant, frictionless operations."[45] At a time of desubjectification and anomy made widespread by the technological means of image production that erases the temporality of an infinite present, Stan Douglas sets himself the task of bringing back to the medium a mnemonic performance in relation to history, figured as an archaeological project of gathering the topologies of biopolitical determinants that, at each crossroads of contemporary history, arrest various forms of life. This second nature, constituted by a disabling politics, reaching us as documentary mass, and is pitched, via re-enactment, alongside a critical revision of the medium and its technical and rhetorical components,

45 Jonathan Crary, *24/7. Late Capitalism and the Ends of Sleep.* London: Verso, 2013, p. 29.

as a process that transports each image to its radical, historical status of having-taken-place, to its own intelligibility, which is also the place of knowledge in its intrinsic relationship with memory. What may be observed in each of these works is not a diachrony or synchrony of history, but the intervals where the subject and its suspended life produces itself. In the work of Stan Douglas, this interplay between interval and presentation in series performs a pendulum motion of rescue, producing in second nature a visibility capable of reinstating an emancipatory critique. To the extent that it brings together two distinct moments in time, this distance is interpretive, and emerges from the order of the very interval as temporal fracture. These two temporalities cannot be thought without this notion, under penalty of being considered symbolic structures, the mystifications of second nature. For this reason, interval becomes the time between their return and its fracturing, coming back with a difference. That this reversibility of images might bring us back not only to history itself, but also to its interregnum, as is the case with *Luanda–Kinshasa*, *The Secret Agent* and *Disco Angola*, and that the potentiality it encapsulates might be visualised, constitutes the politics of the mediums themselves. The contribution of Stan Douglas lies in the dimension of play which he submits these elements.

Disco Angola, 2012

8 digital C-print mounted on Dibond aluminium
Edition of 5

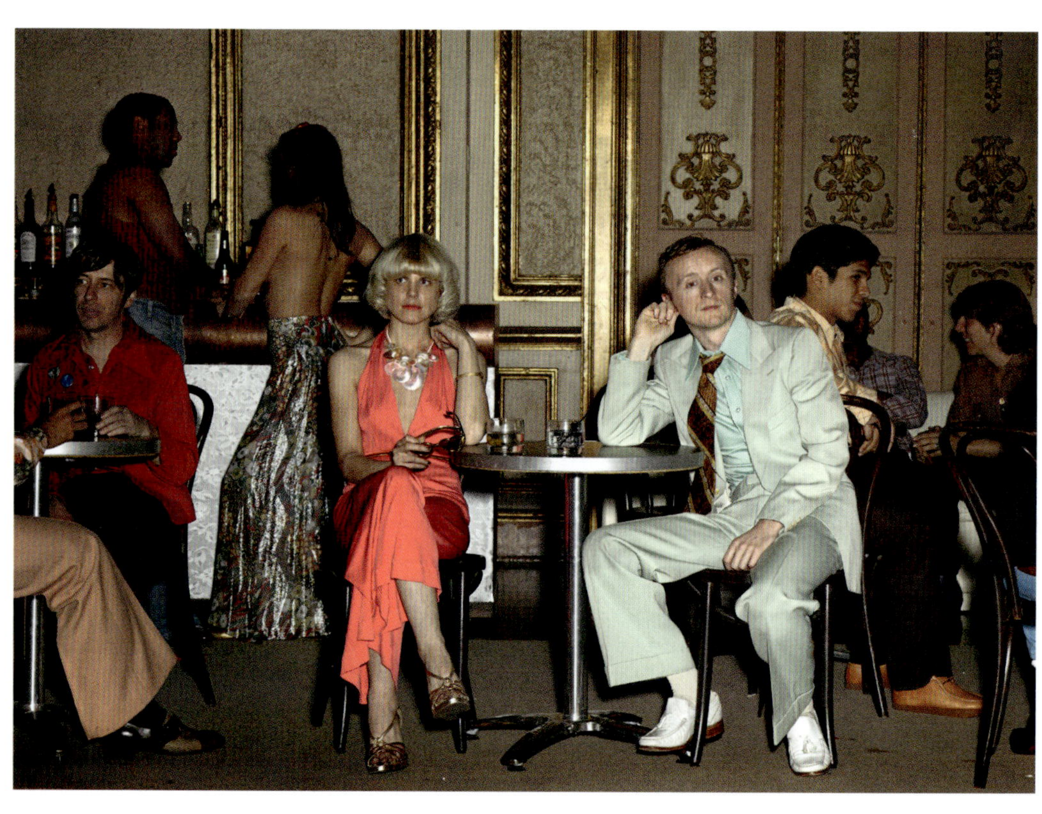

Two Friends, 1975, 2012
108 × 143.5 cm

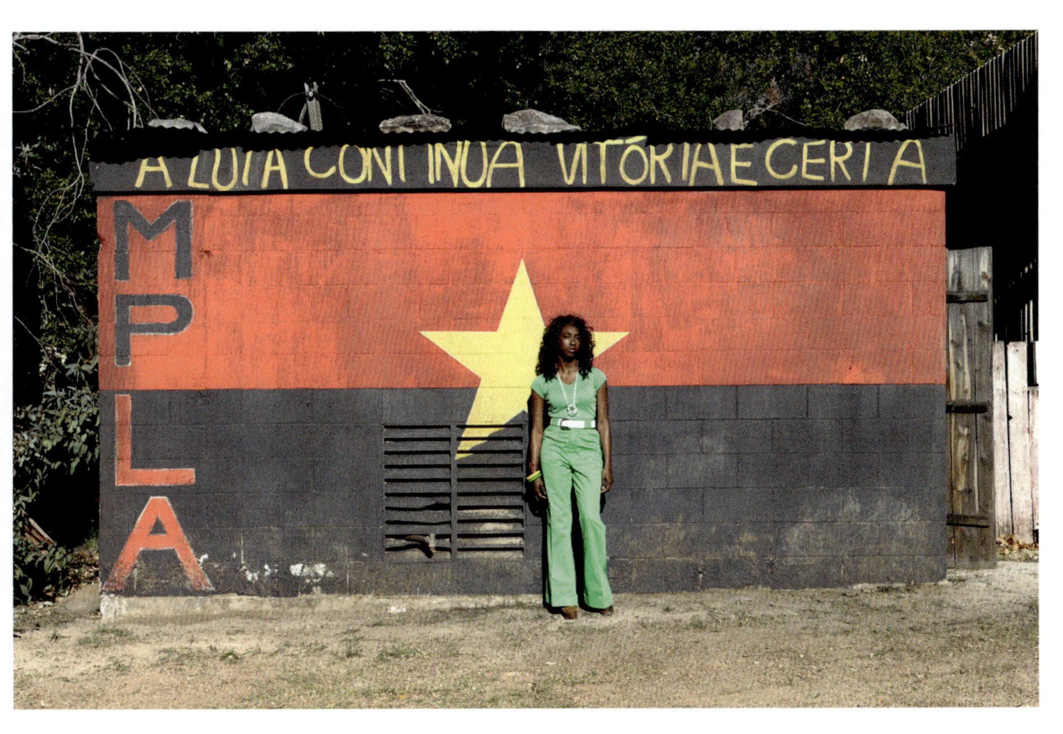

A Luta Continua, 1974, 2012
121.9 × 182.2 cm

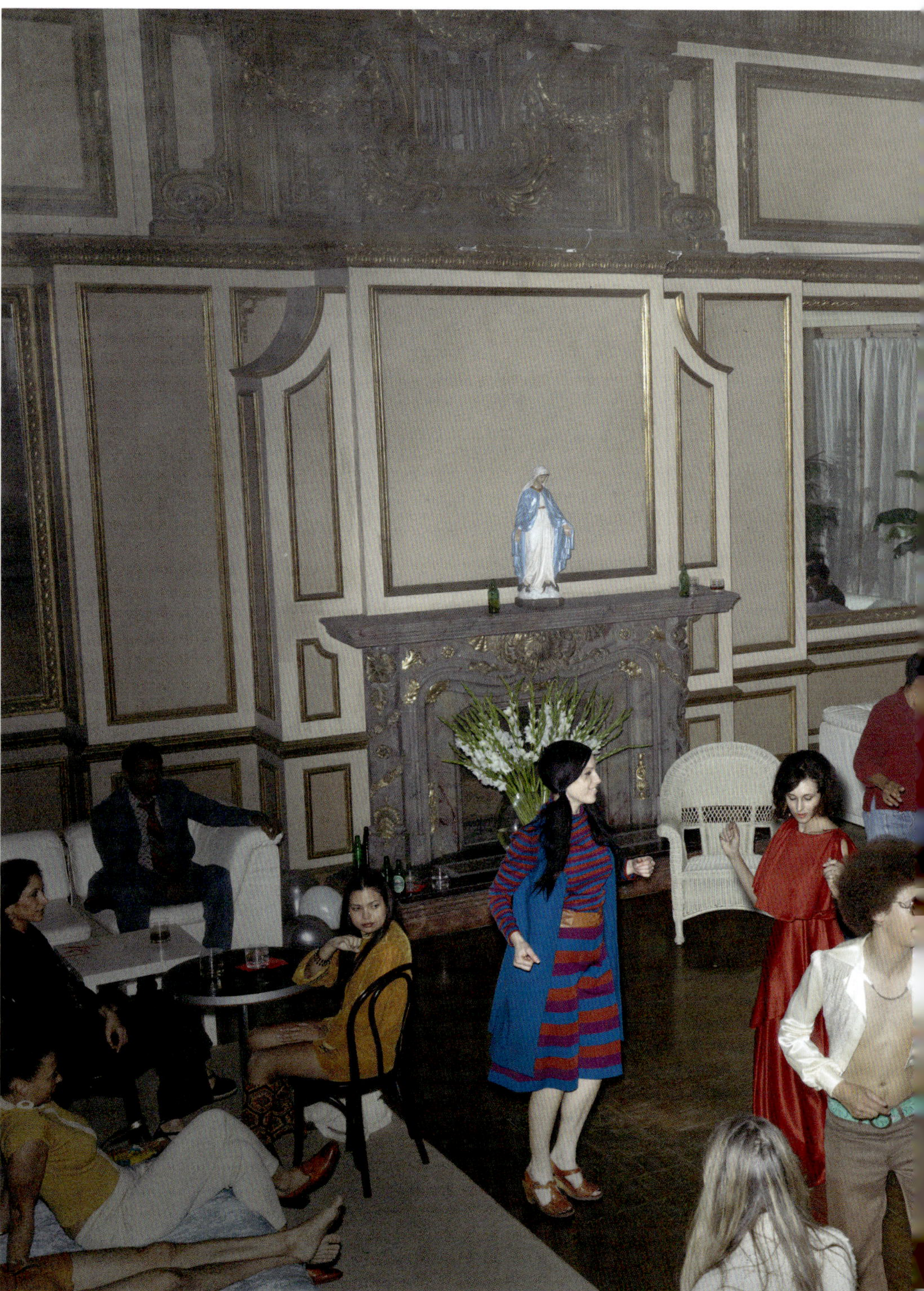

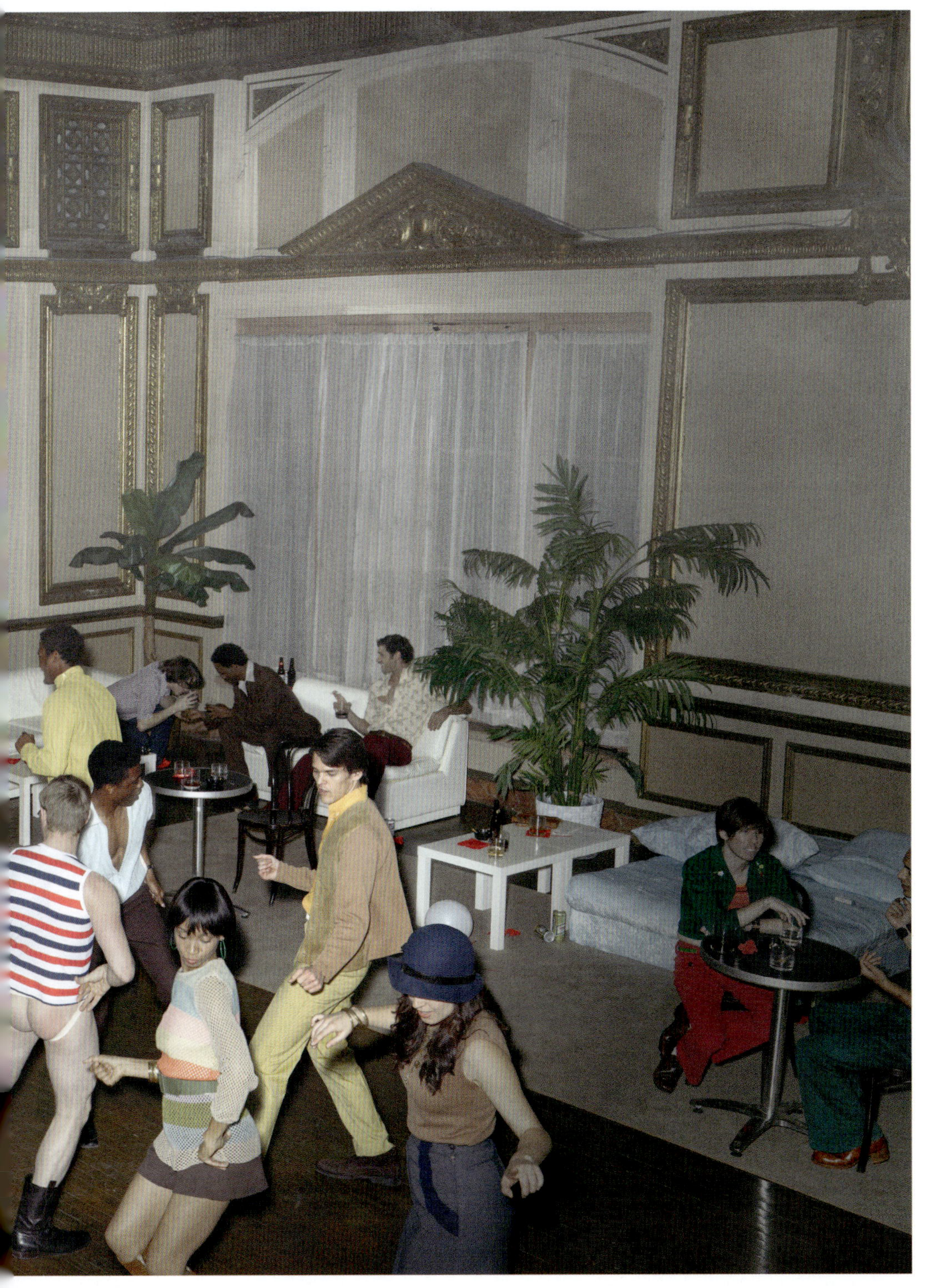

Club Versailles, 1975, 2012
152.4 × 228 cm

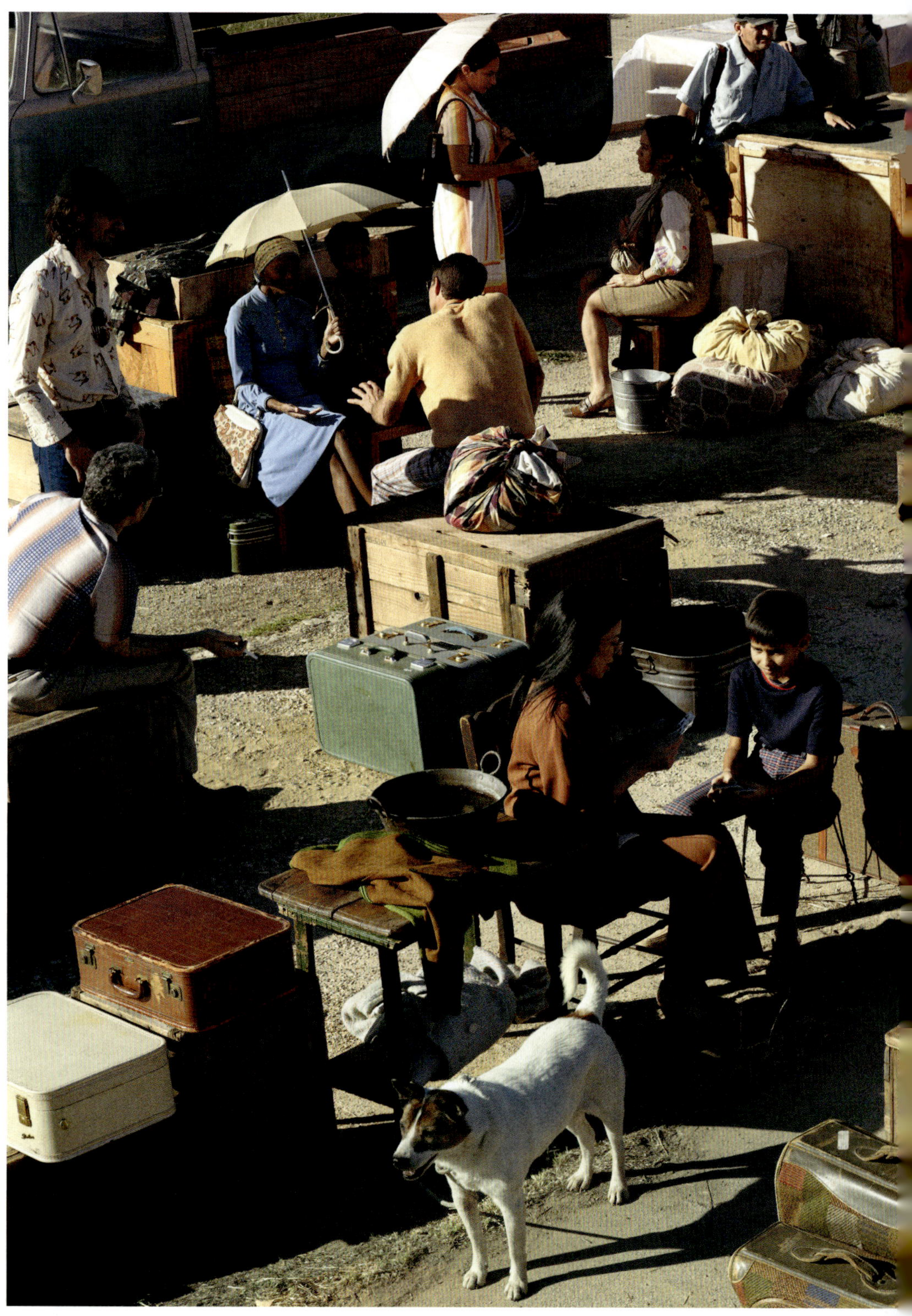

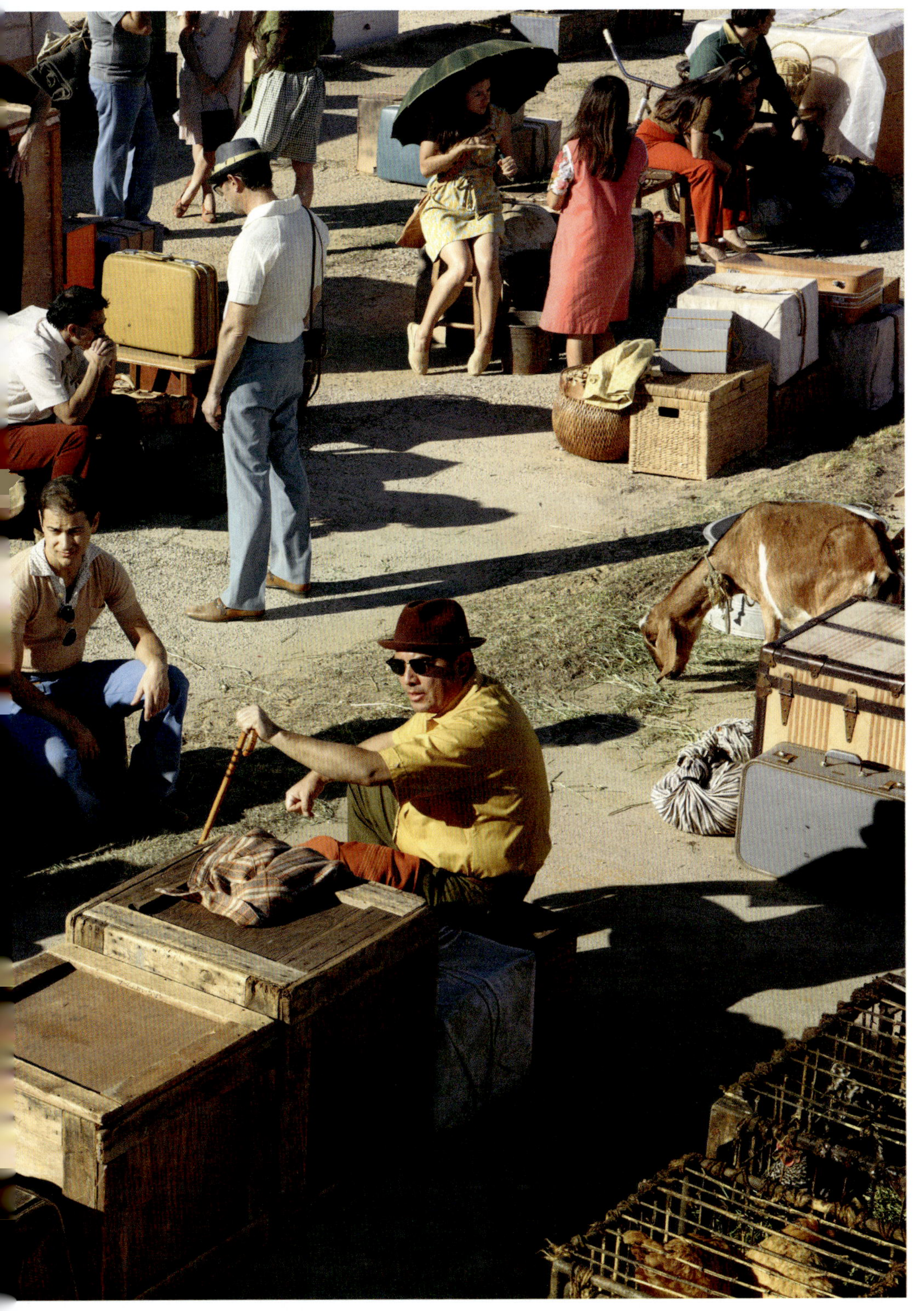

Exodus, 1975, 2012. 181.6 × 259.1 cm

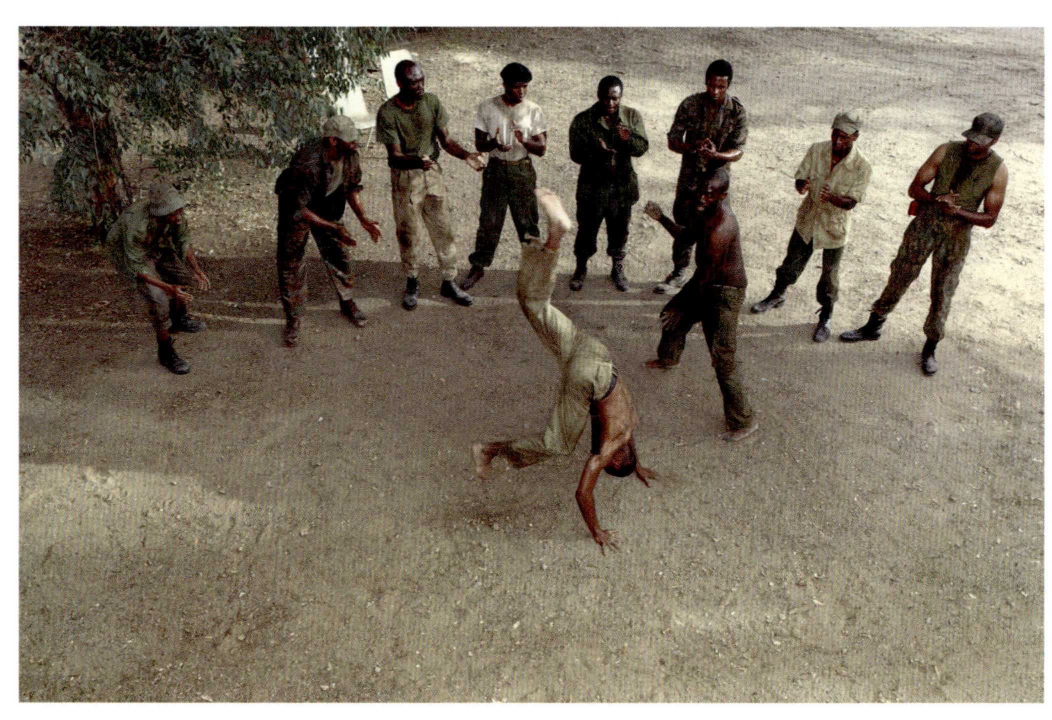

Capoeira, 1974, 2012
143.5 × 214.6 cm

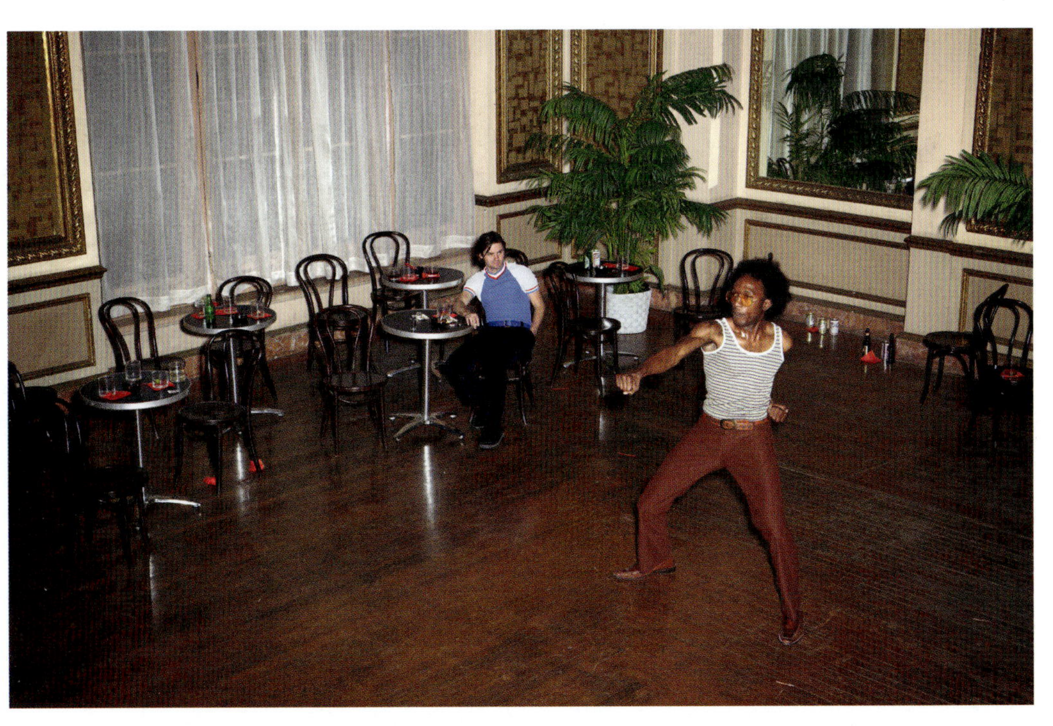

Kung-Fu Fighting, 1975, 2012
92.7 × 138.4 cm

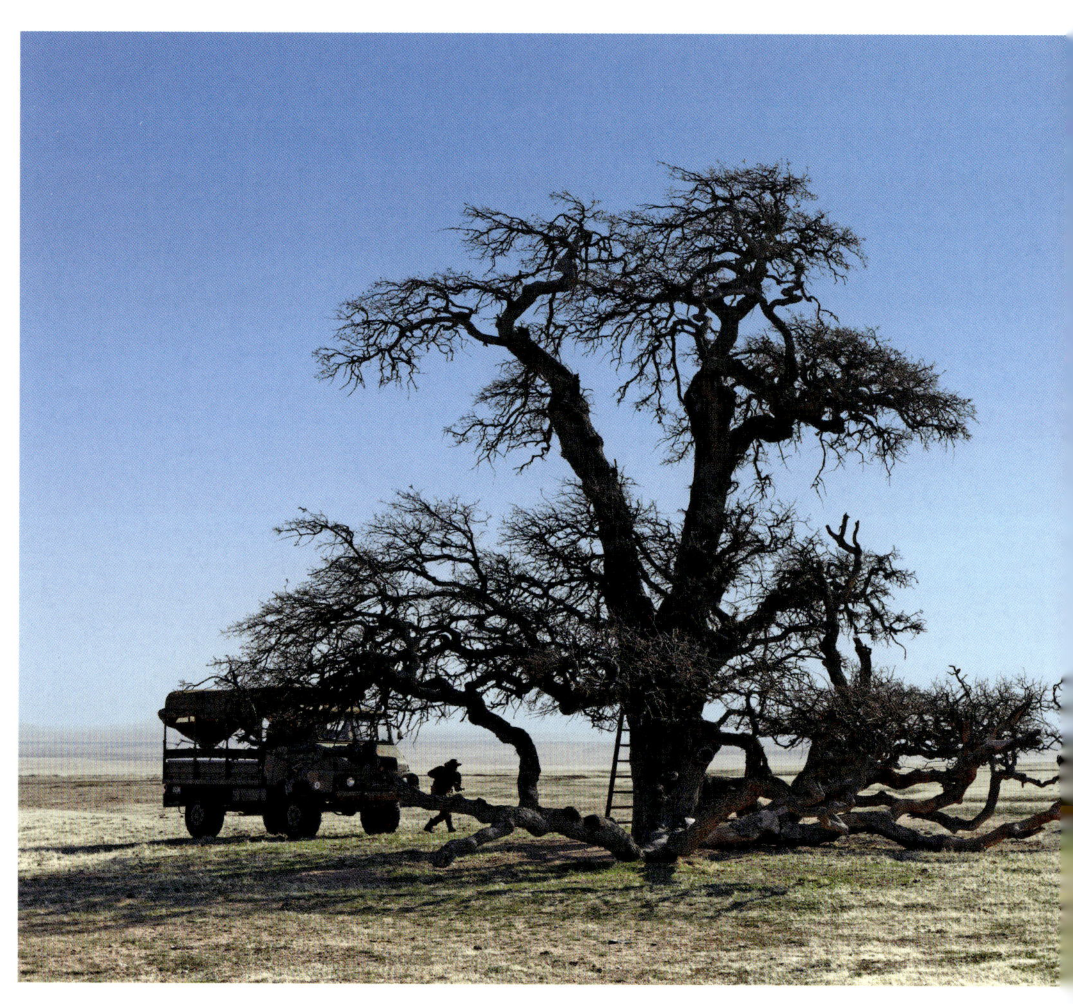

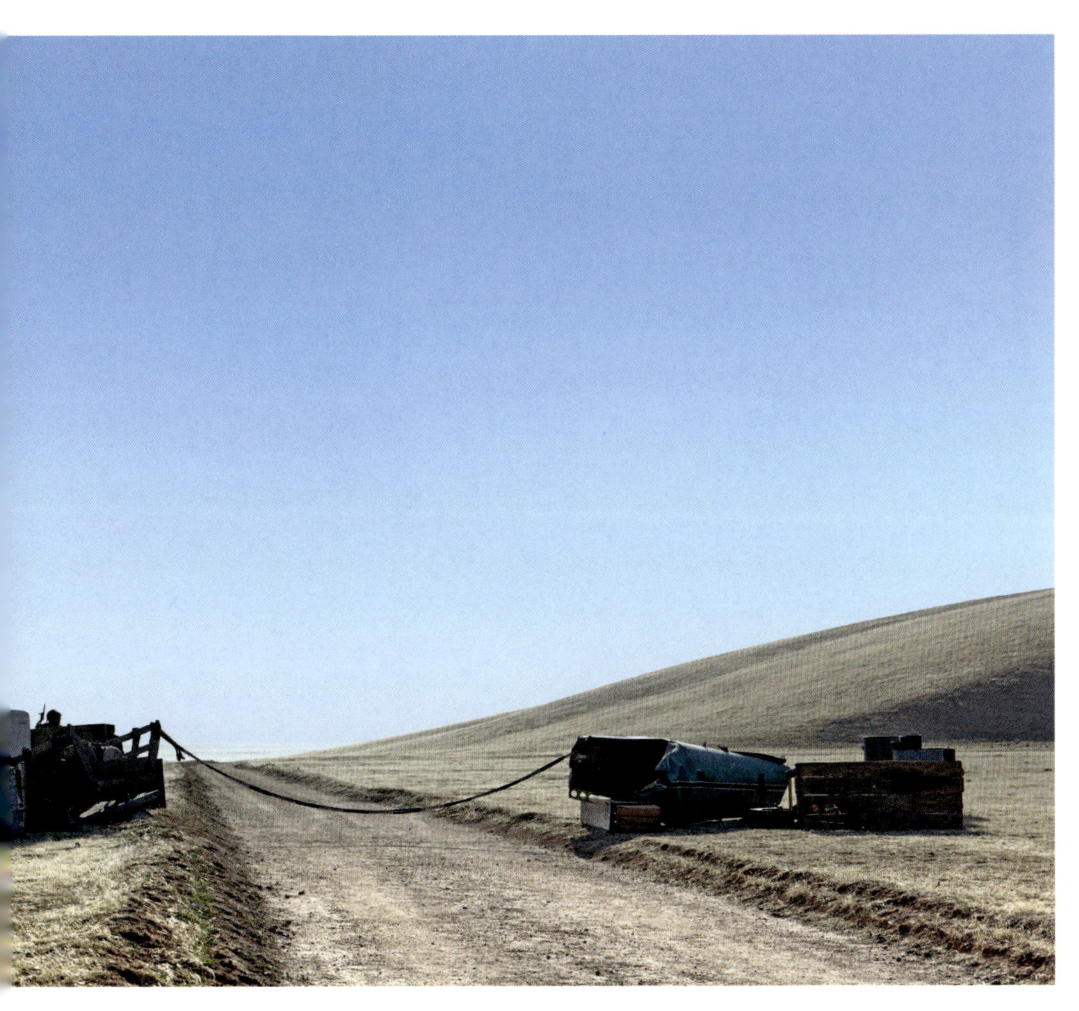

Ceckpoint, 1975, 2012
133.4 × 304.8 cm

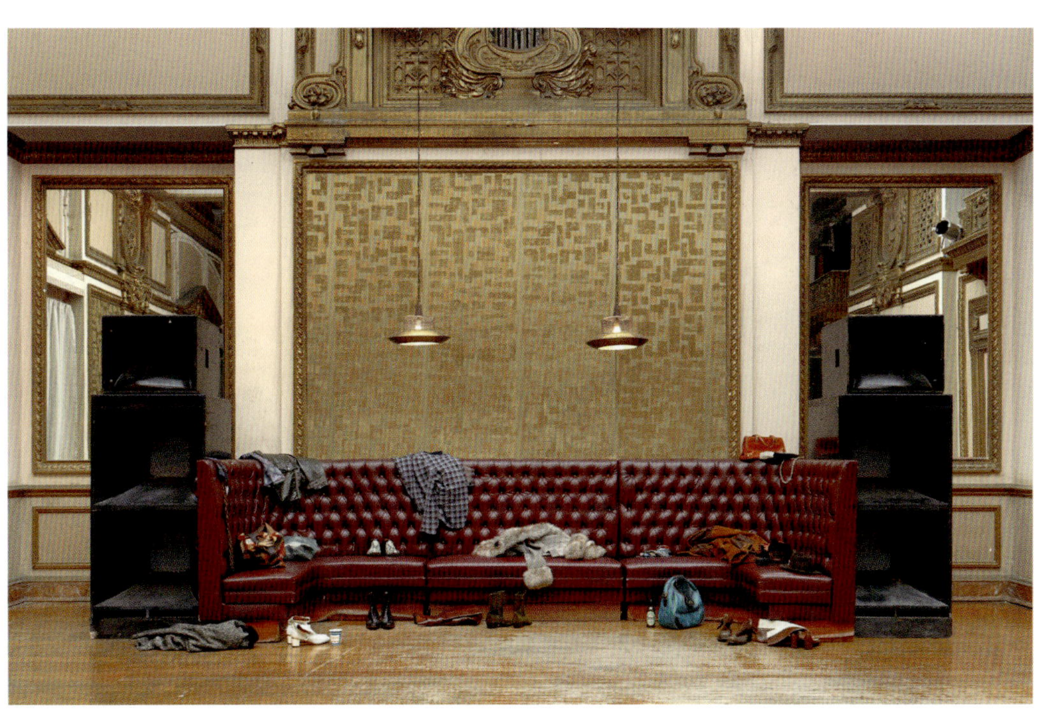

Coat Check, 1974, 2012
121.9 × 182.2 cm

Luanda-Kinshasa, 2013

Single-channel video projection, colour, sound;
6 hours and 1 minute, loop
Overall dimensions vary with installation
(aspect ratio 4:3)
Edition of 4

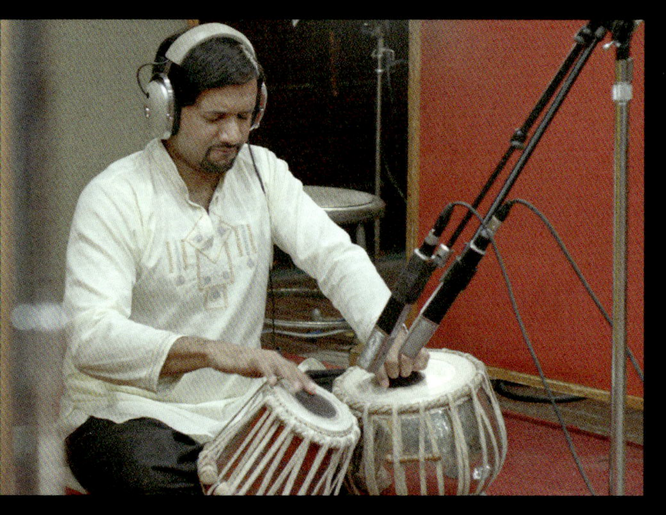
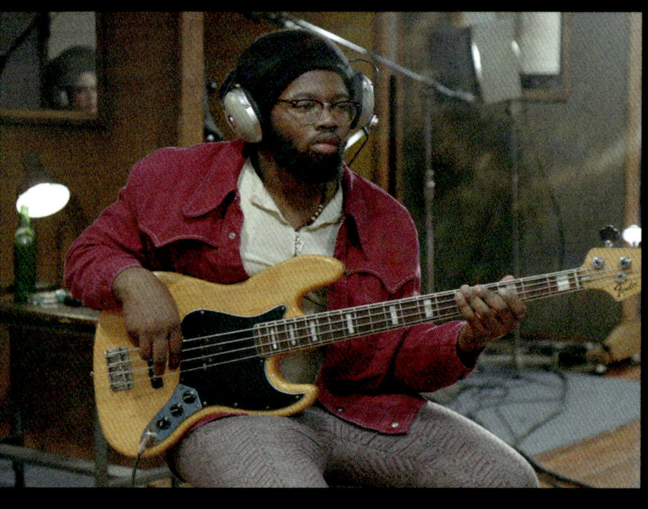
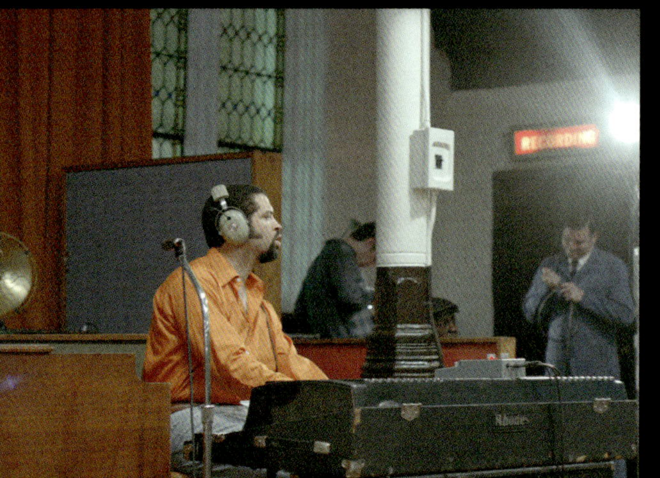

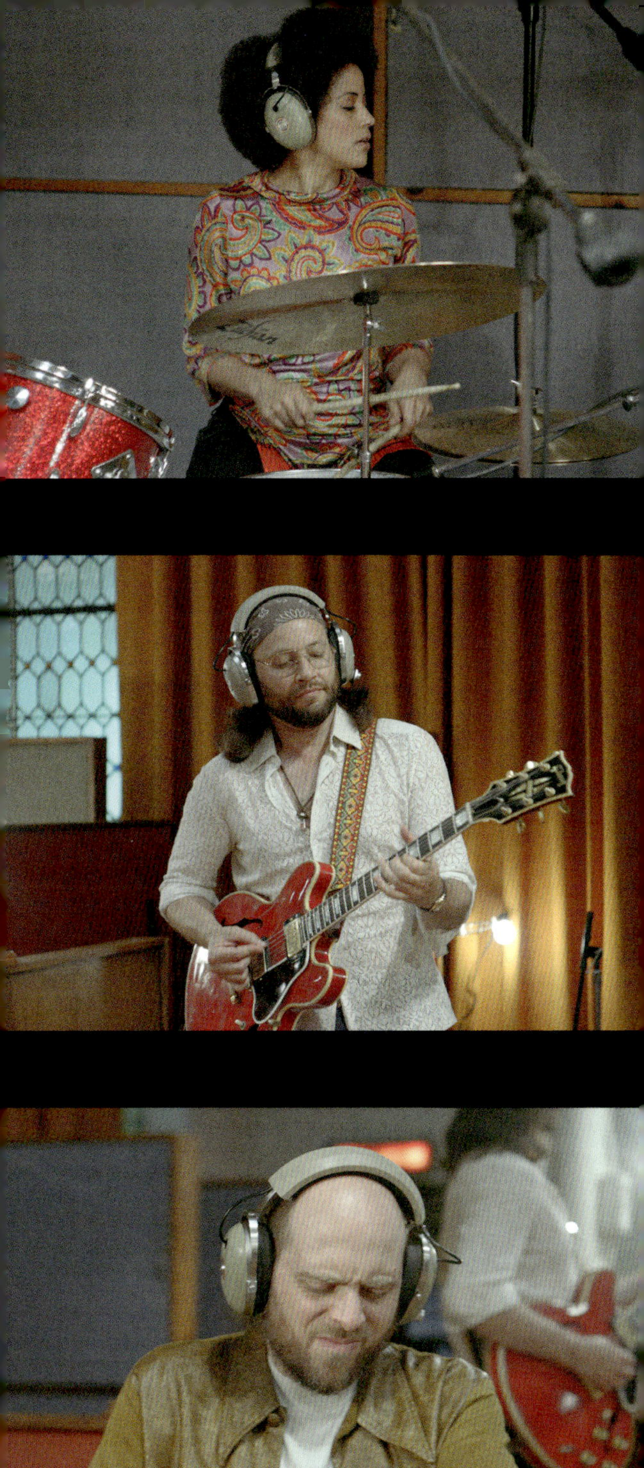

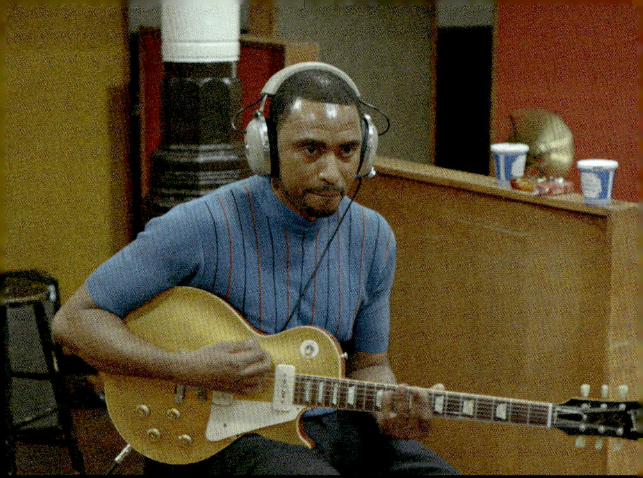

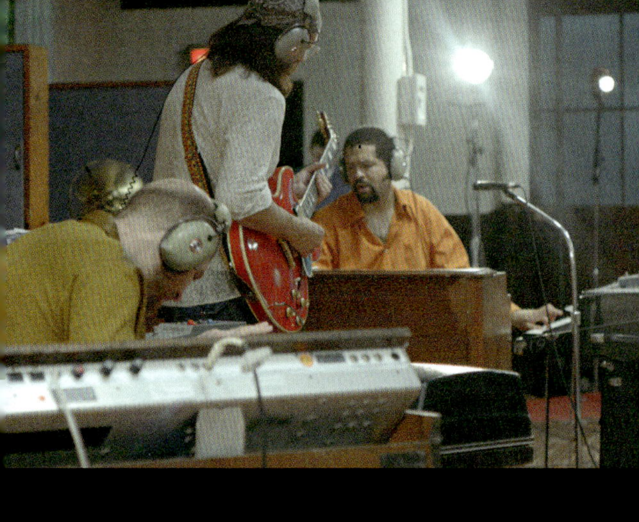
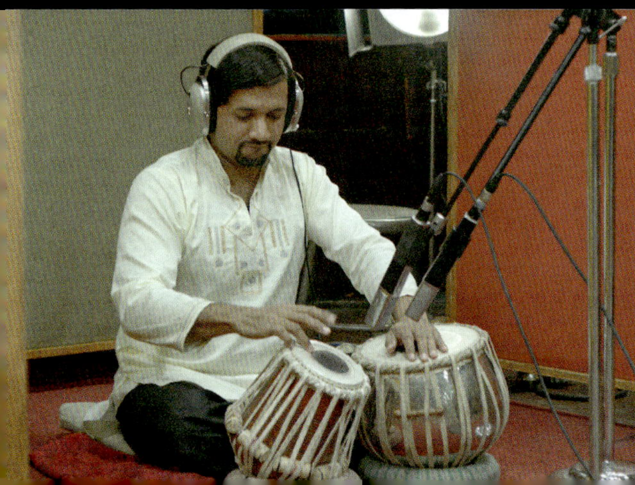

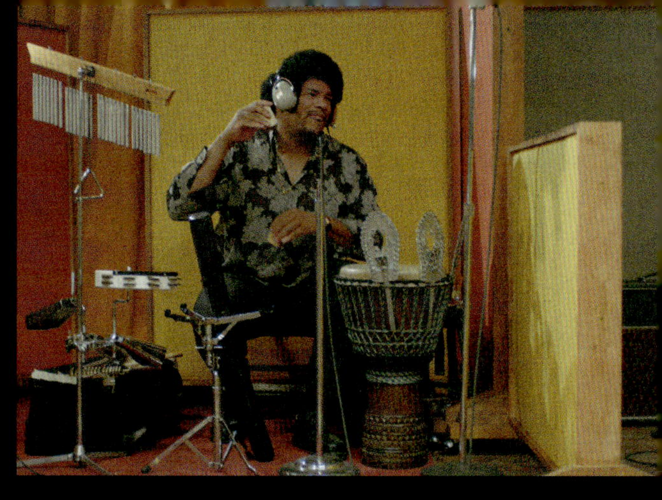

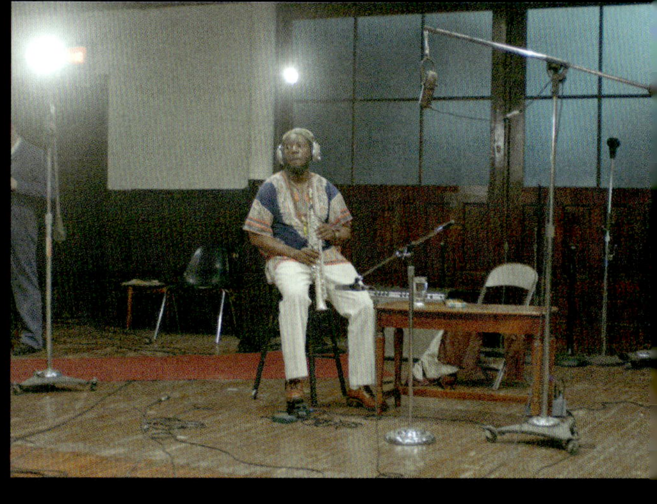

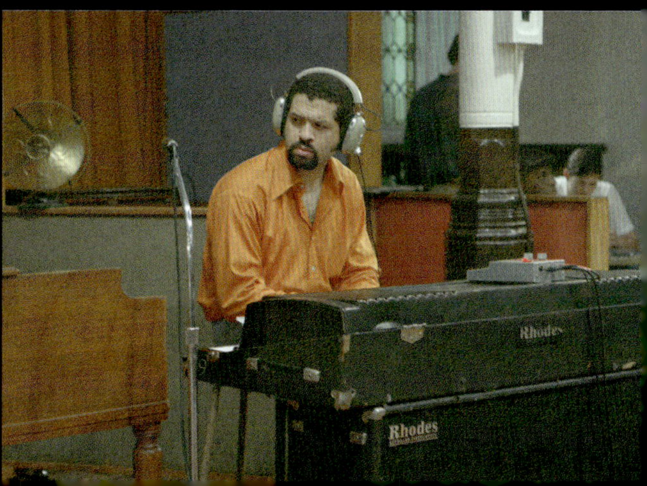

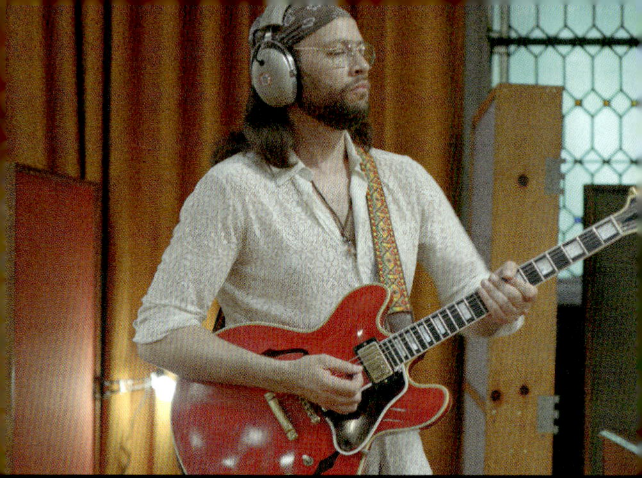

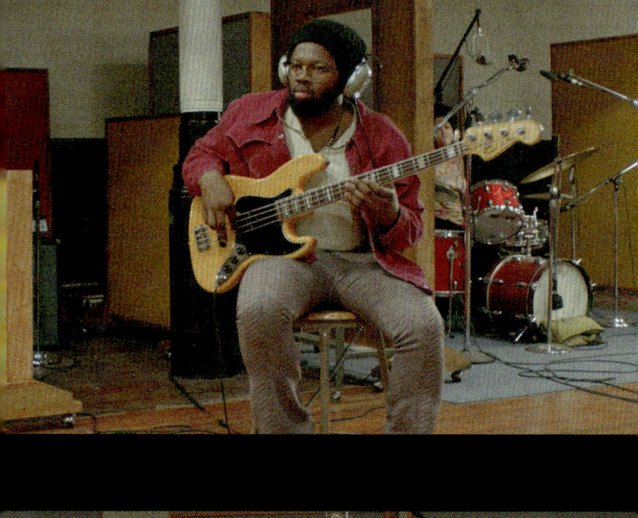
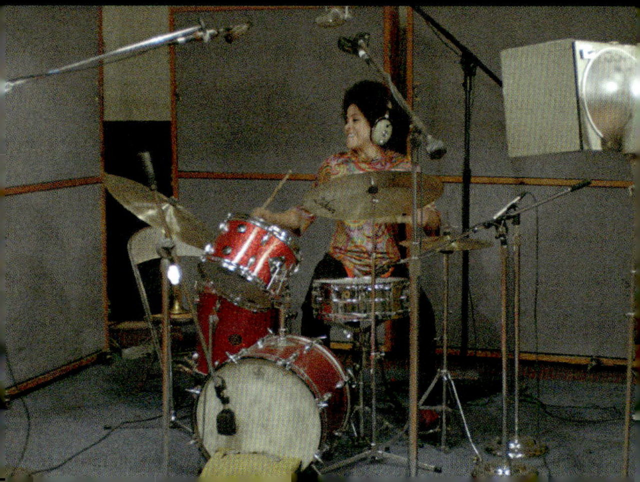

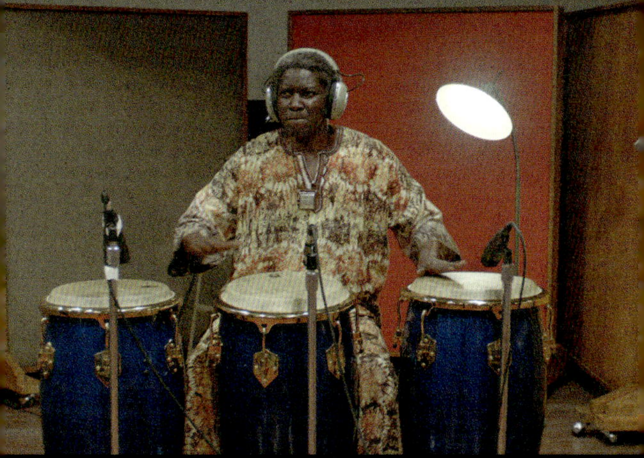

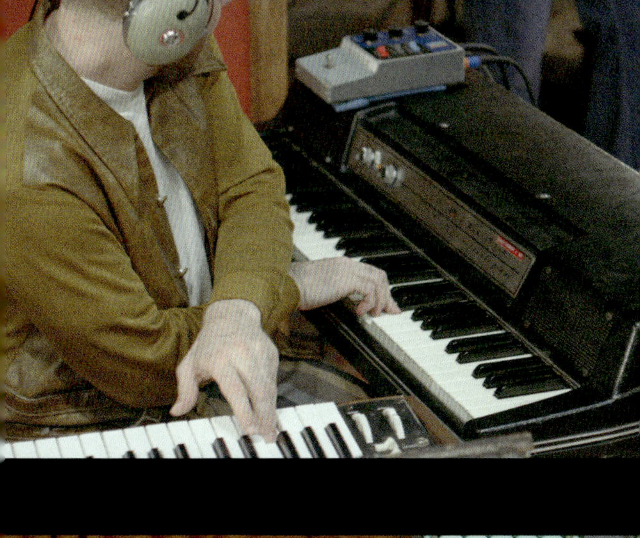
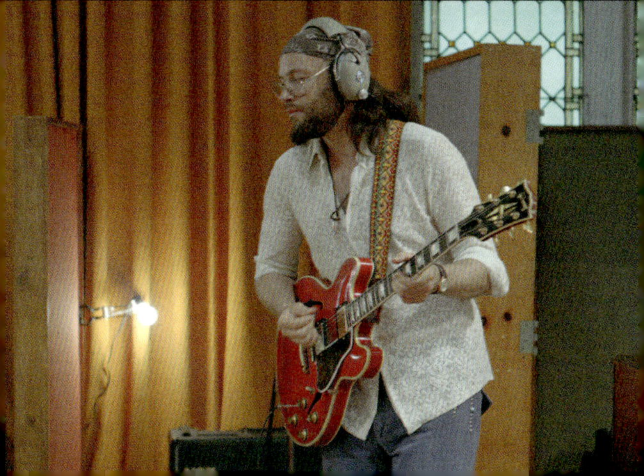

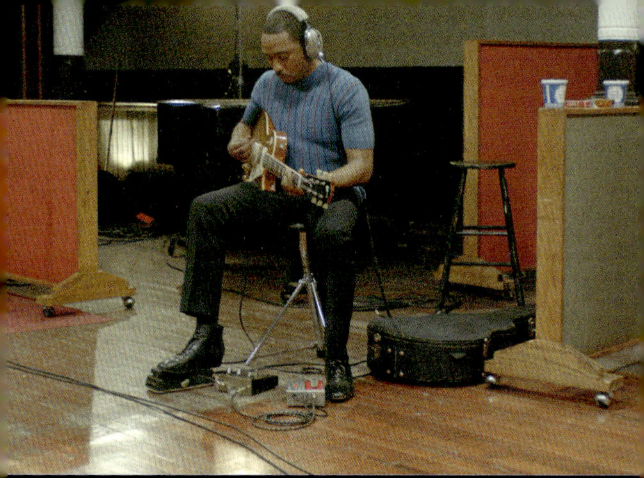

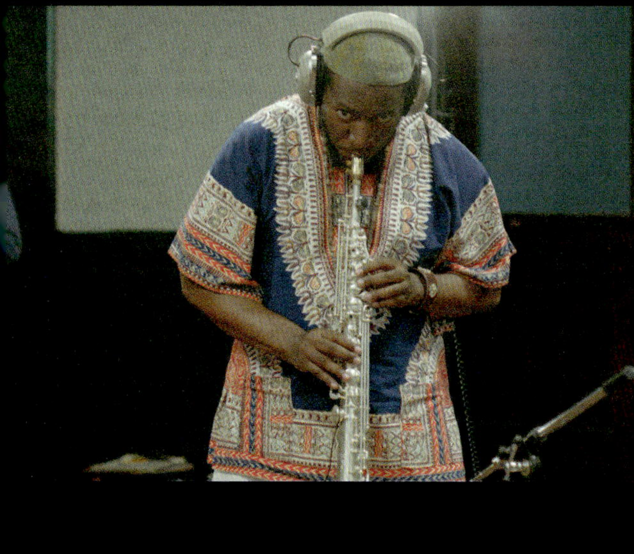

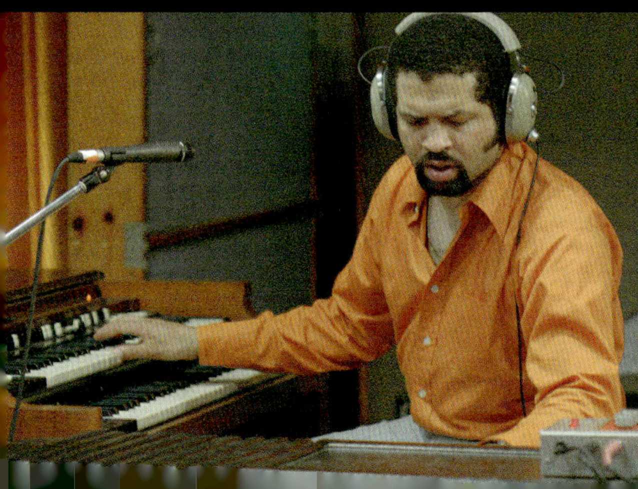

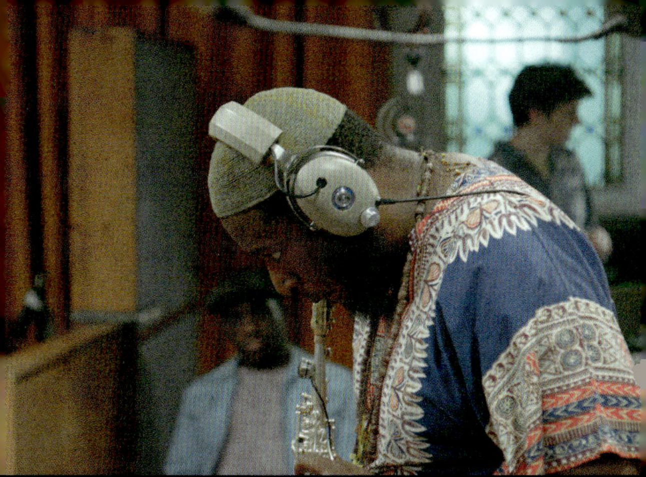

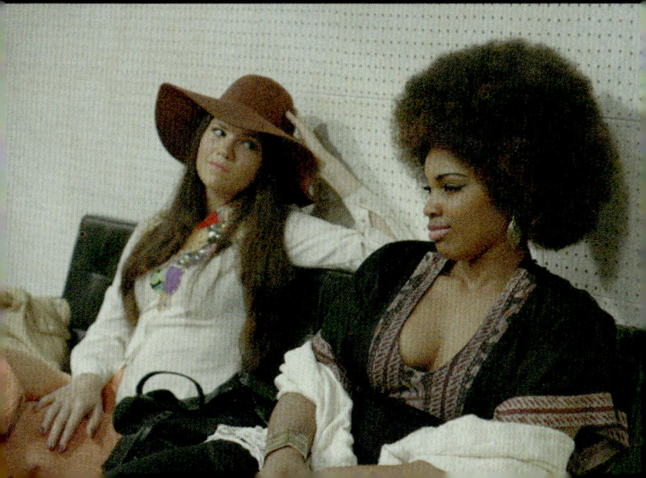

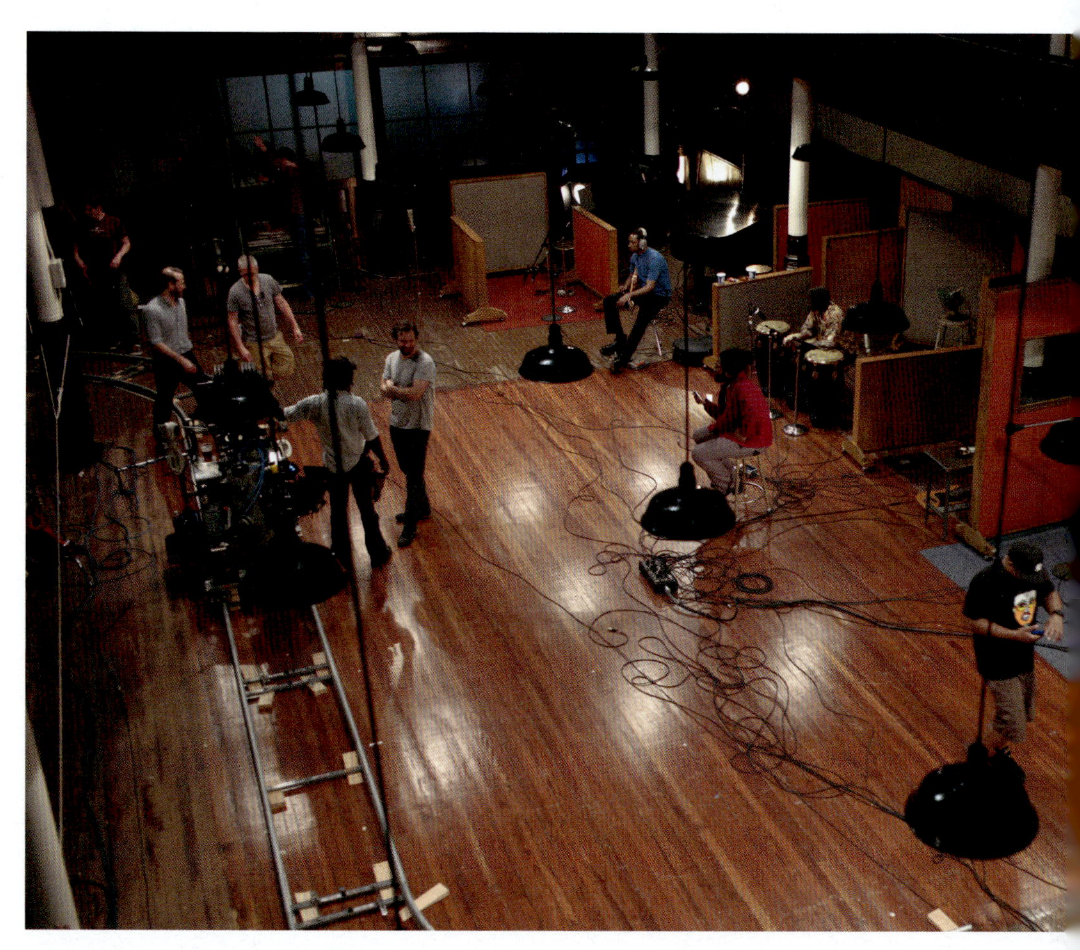

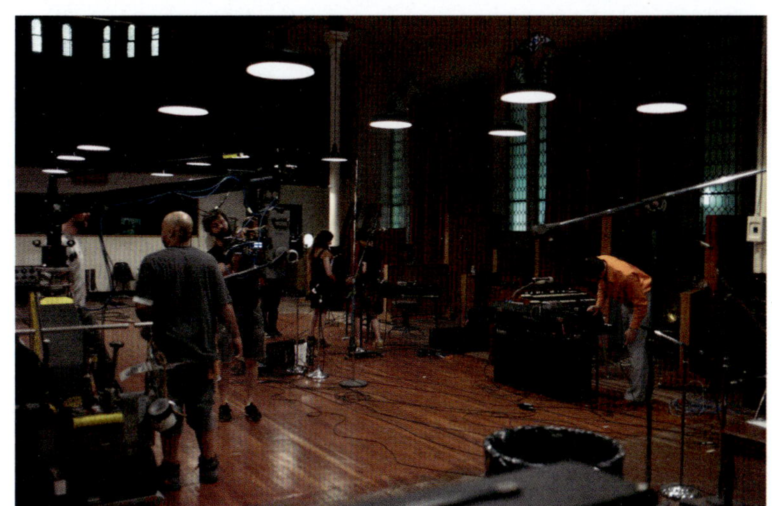

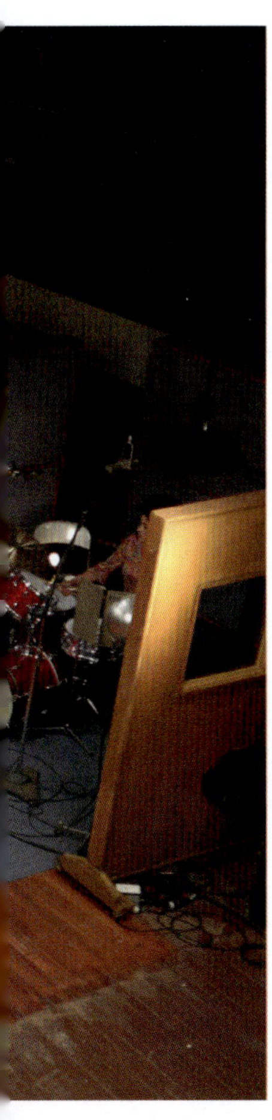

Luanda-Kinshasa, 2013
Production photographs by Stan Douglas

The Secret Agent, 2015

Six-channel video installation,
eight audio channels, colour, sound;
53 minutes and 35 seconds, loop
(with eight musical variations)
Overall dimensions vary with installation
(aspect ratio 4:3)
Edition of 4

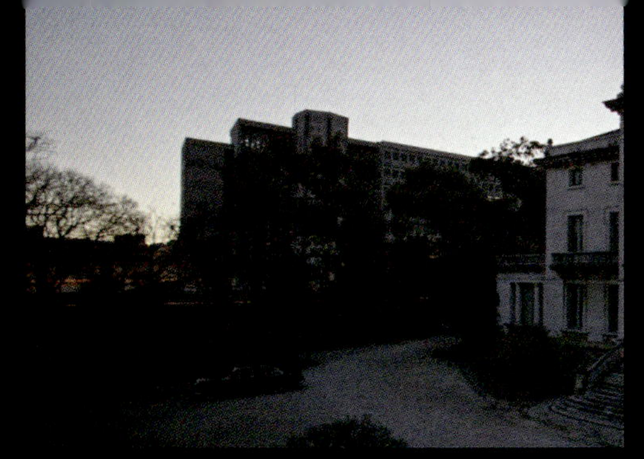
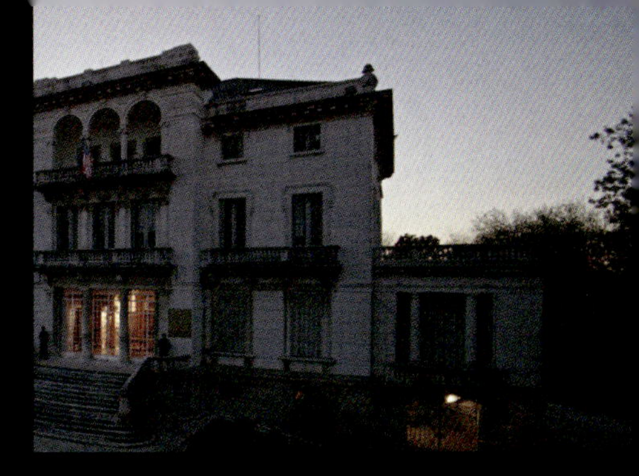
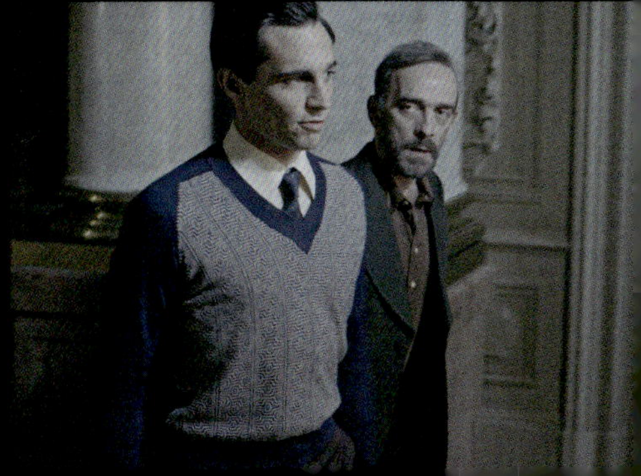

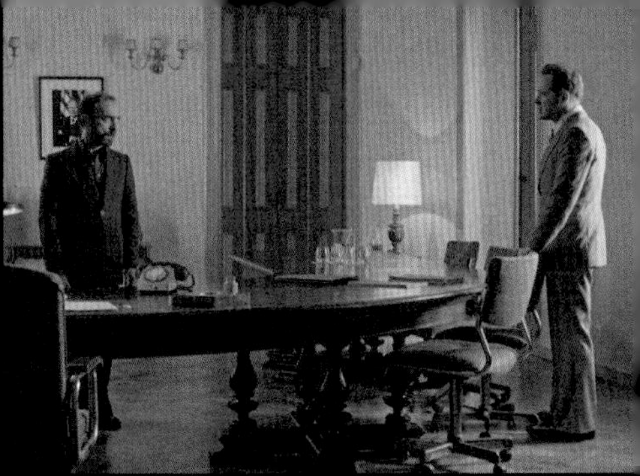

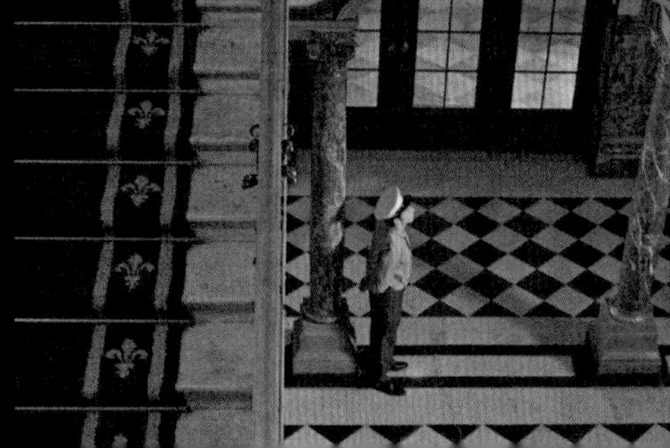

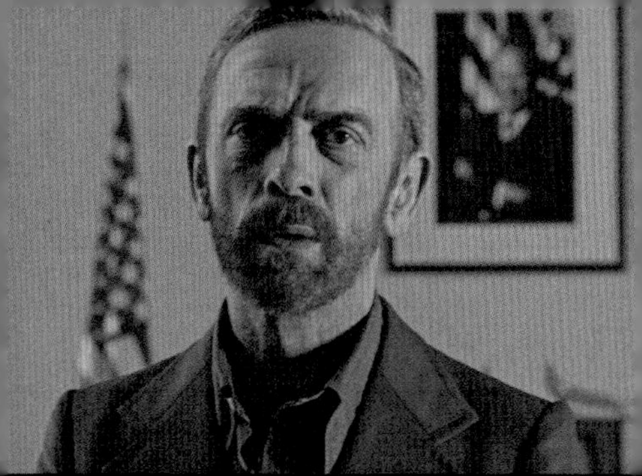

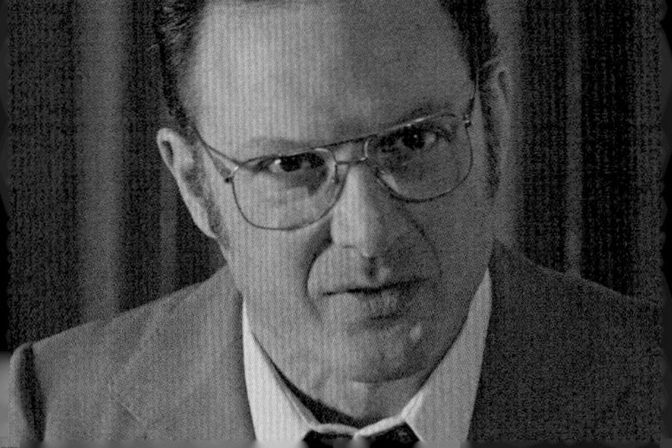

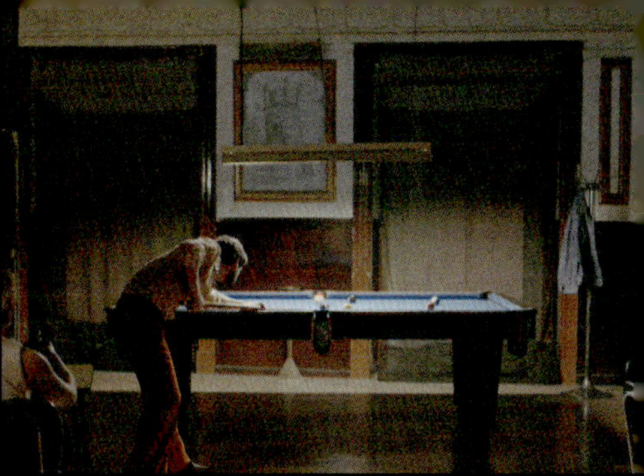

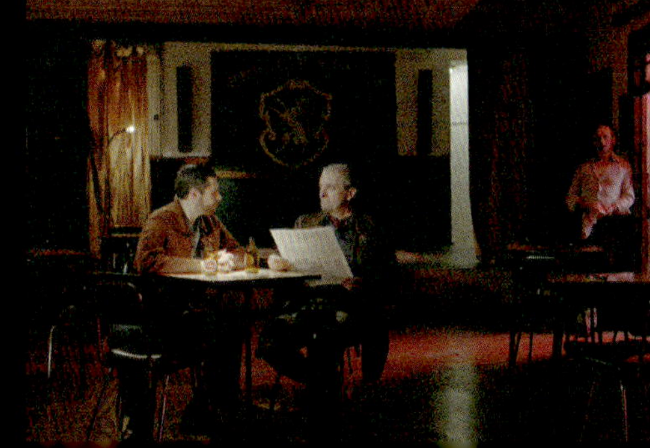

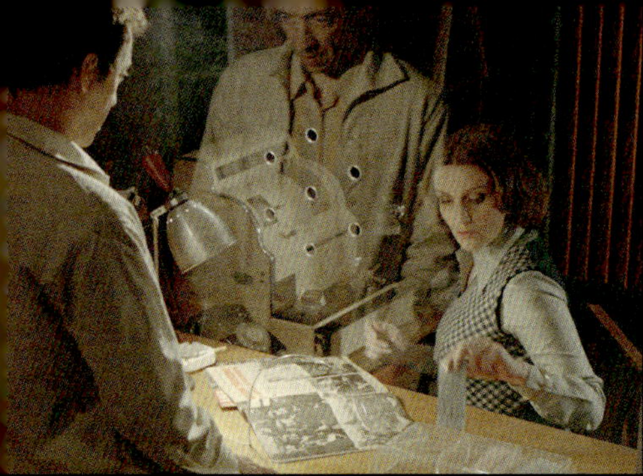

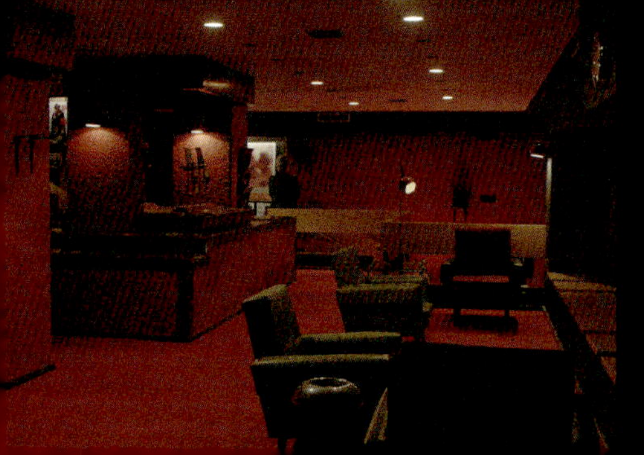

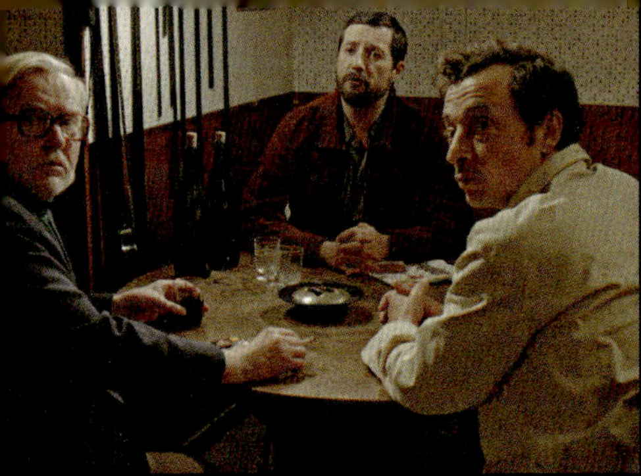

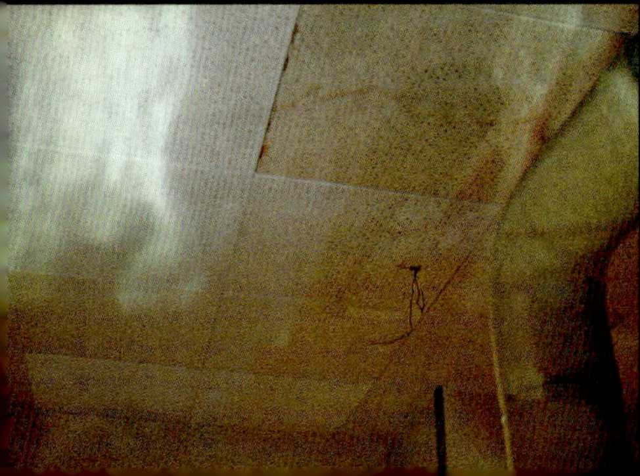

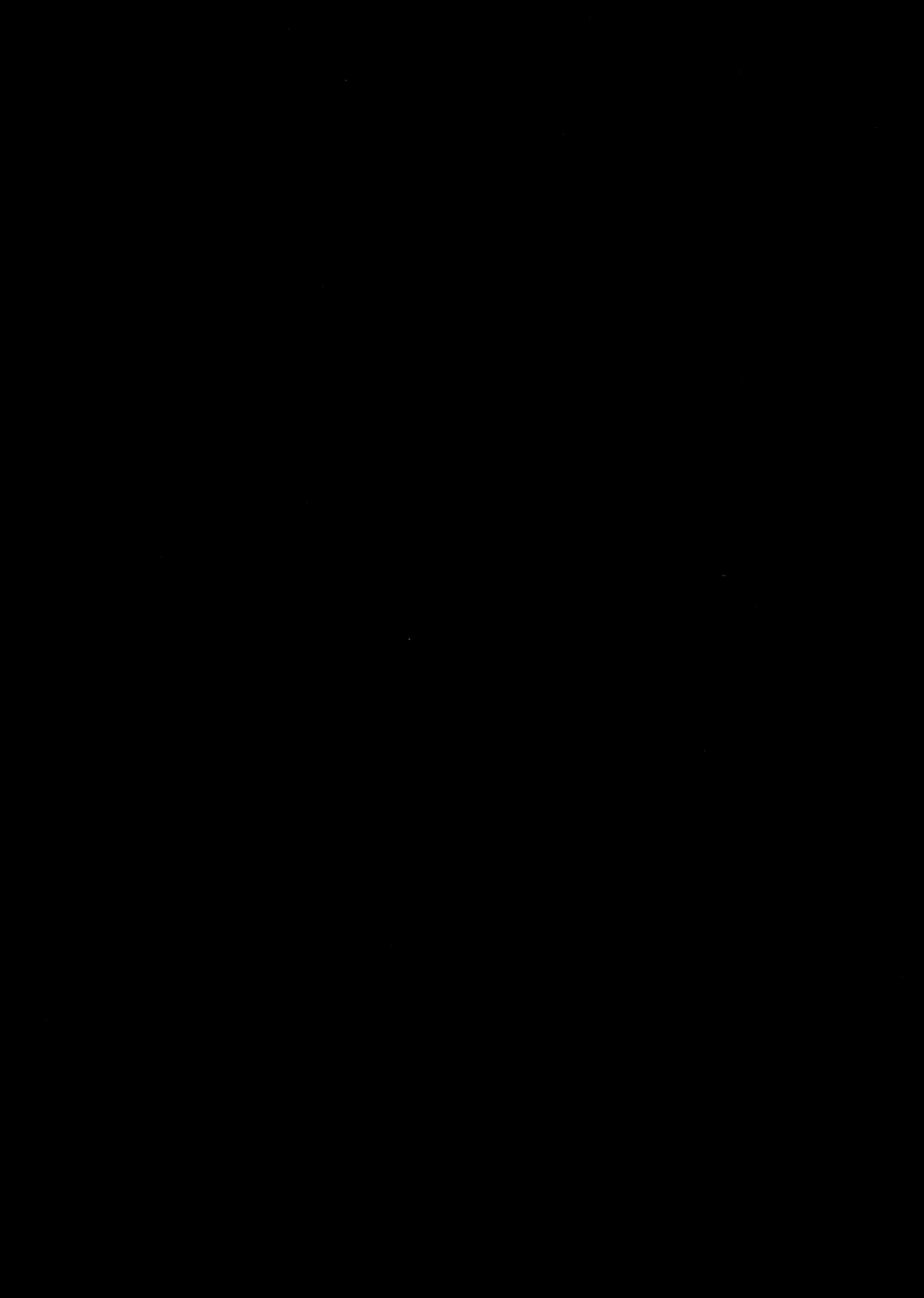

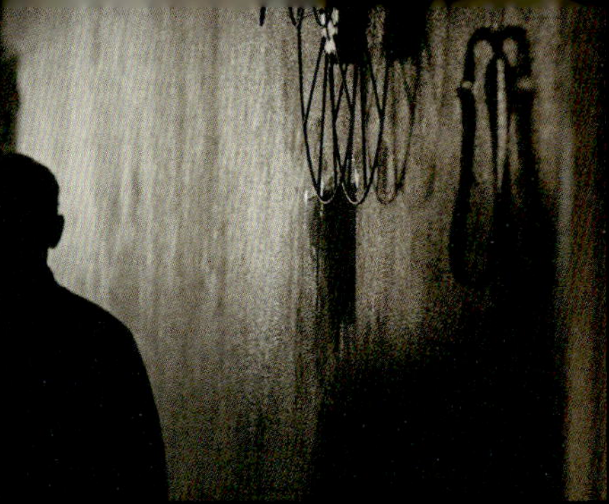

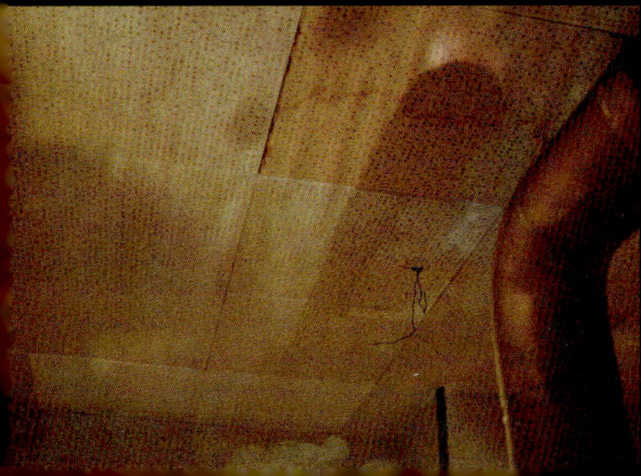

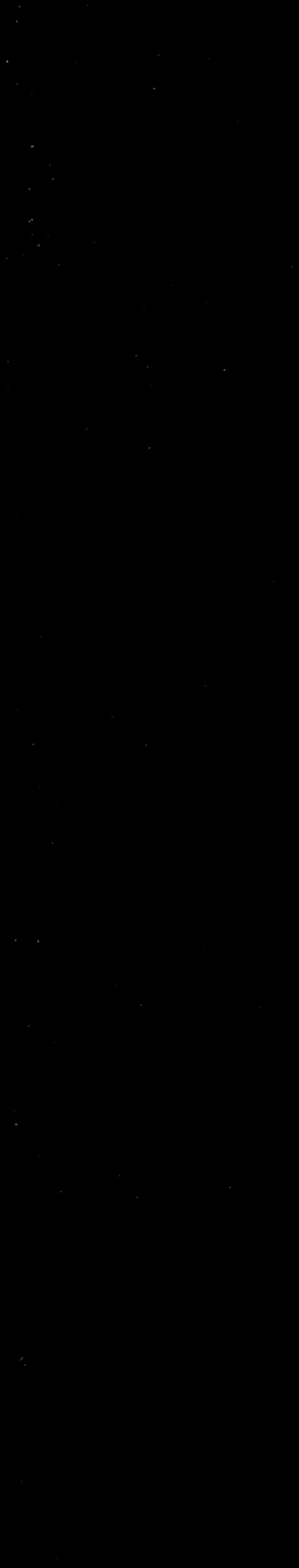

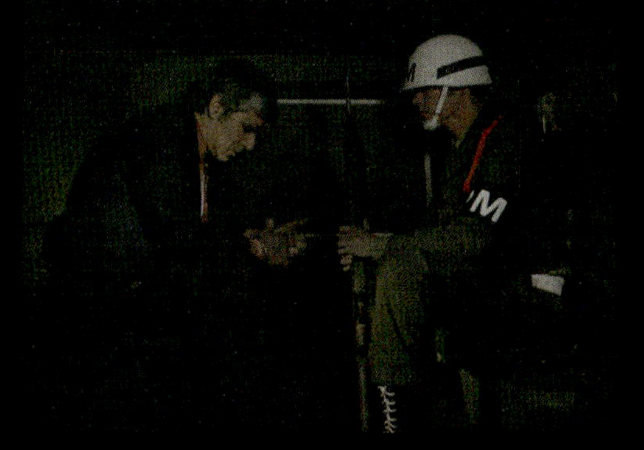

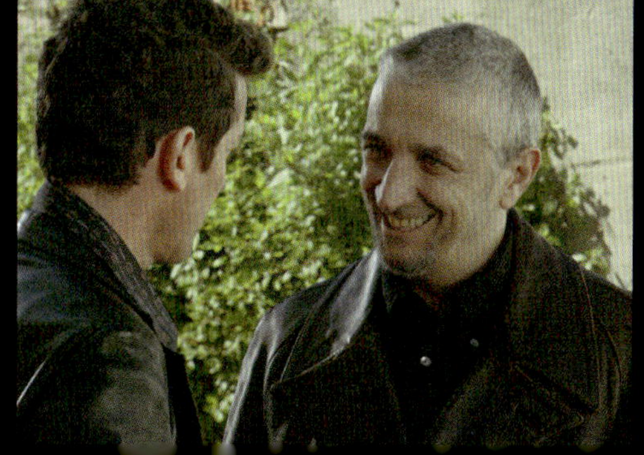

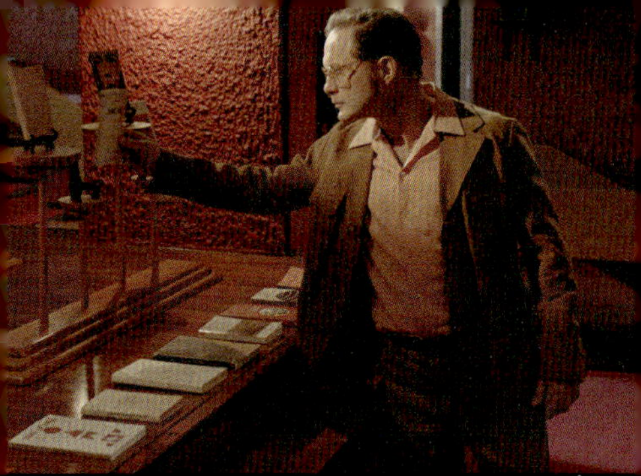

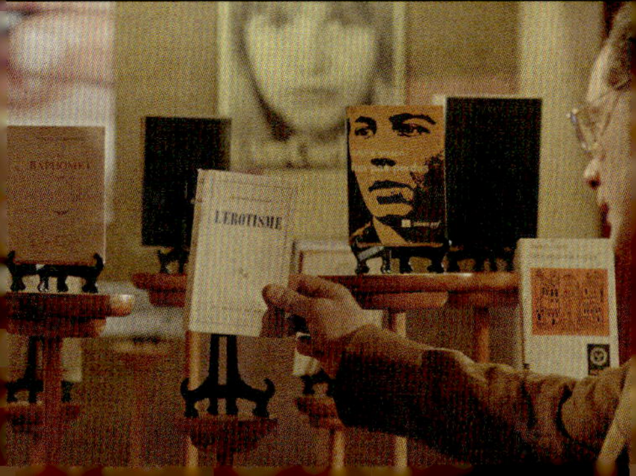

L'EROTISME

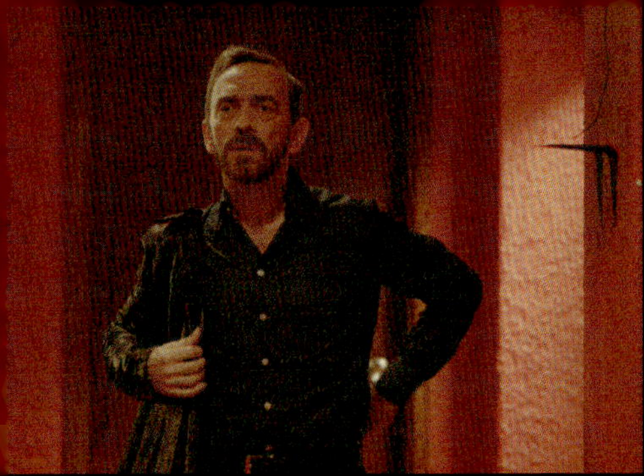

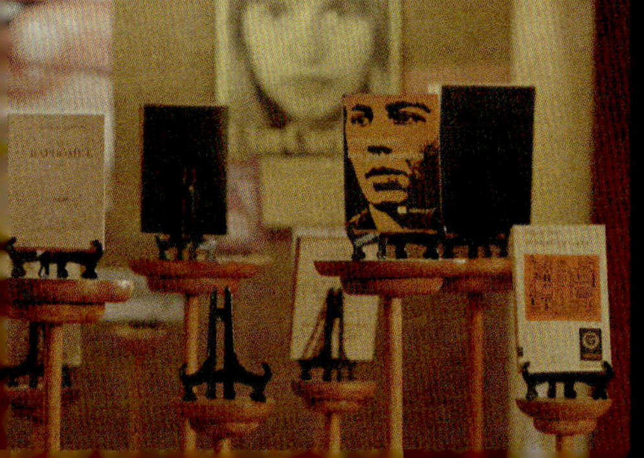

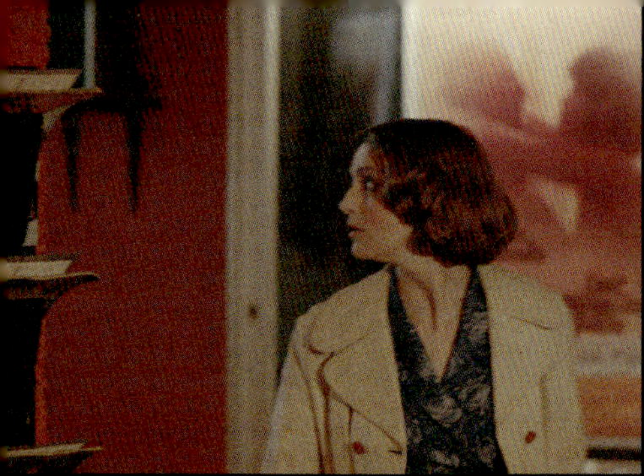

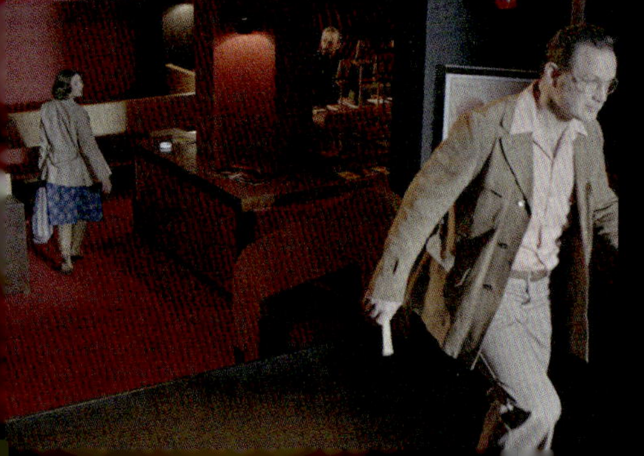

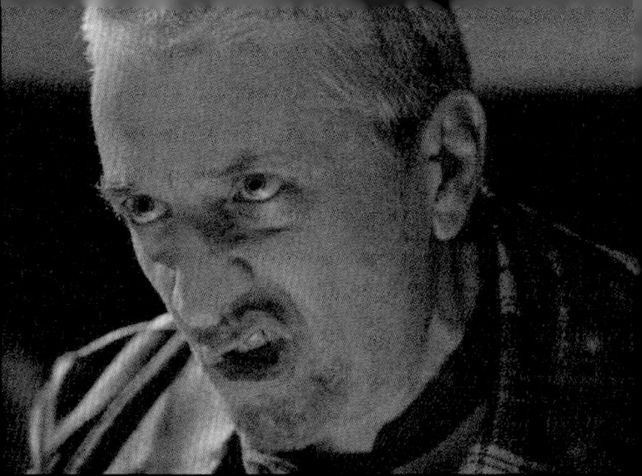

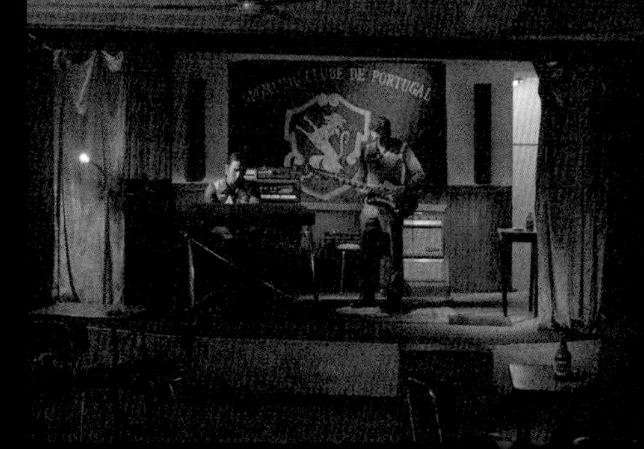
CLUBE DE PORTUGAL

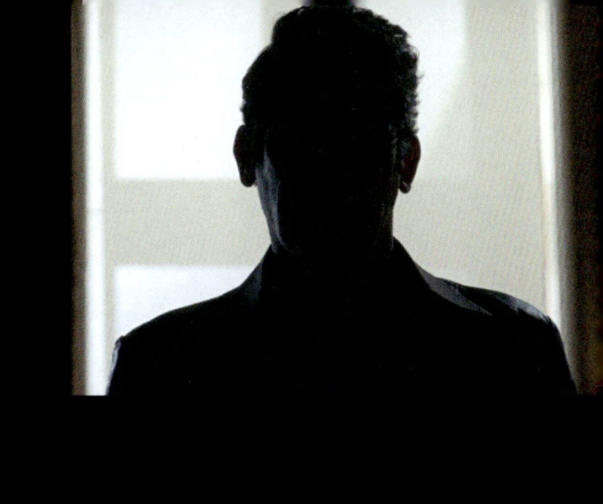

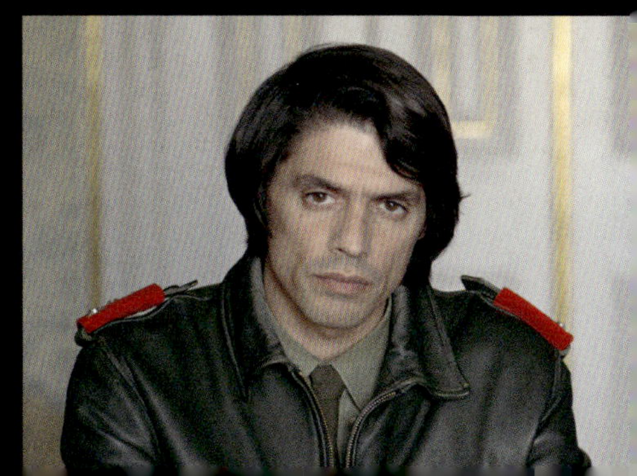

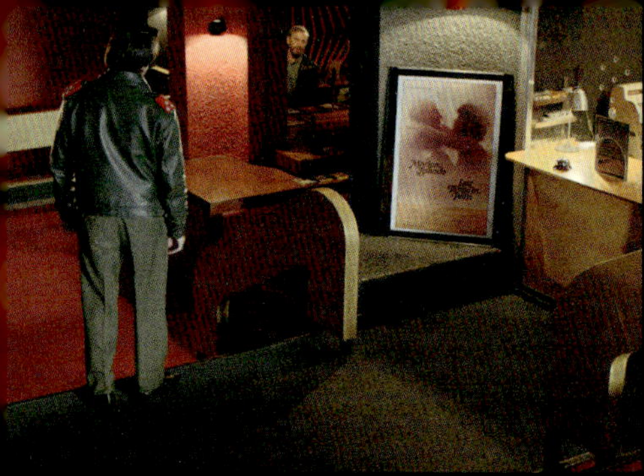

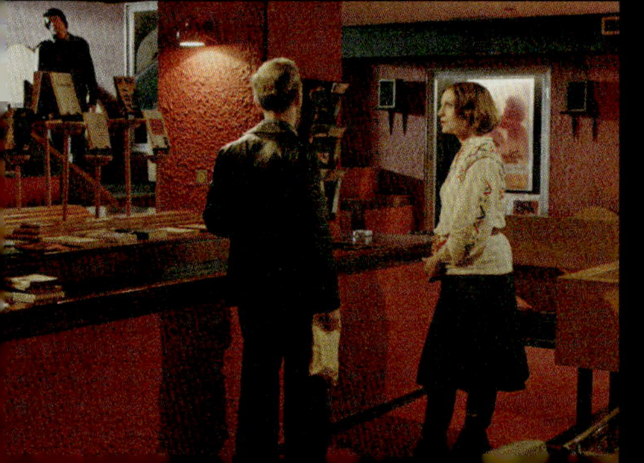

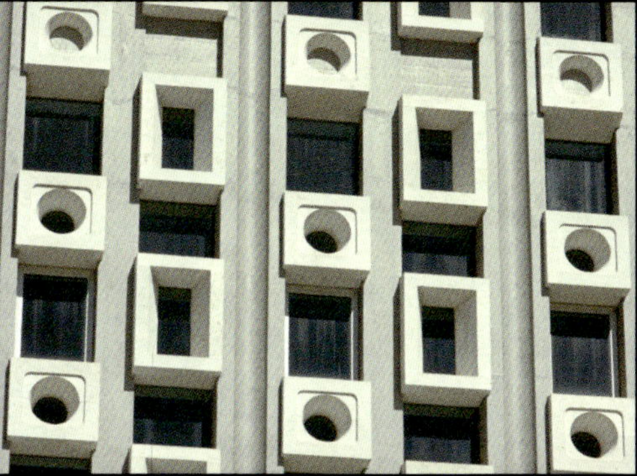

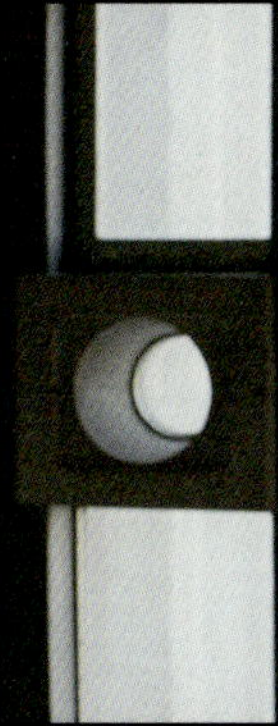

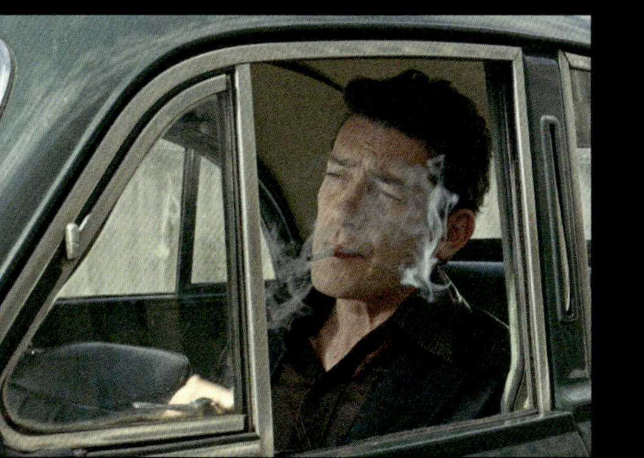

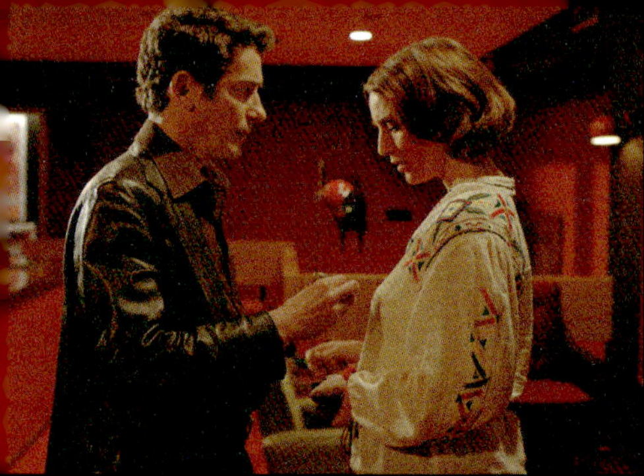

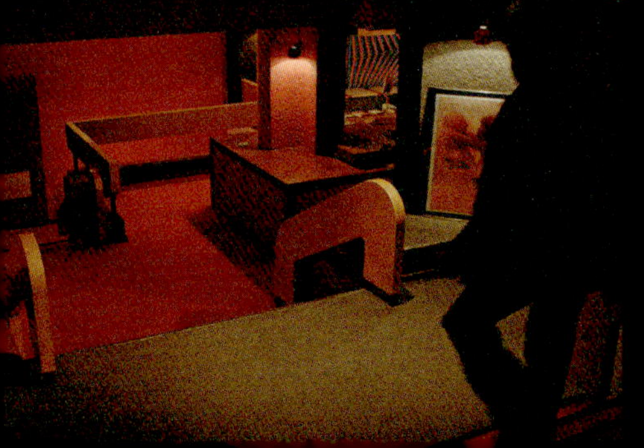

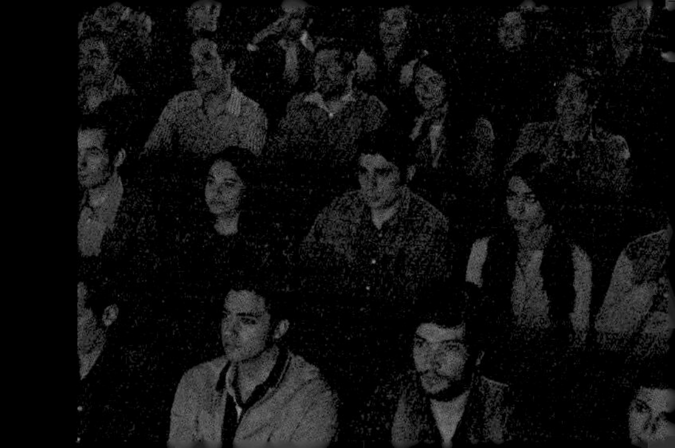

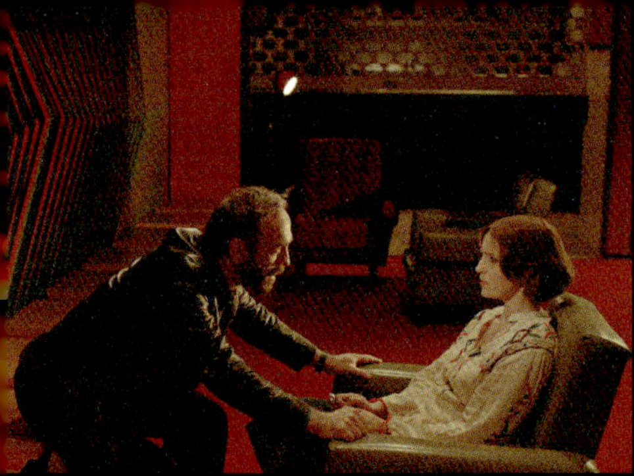

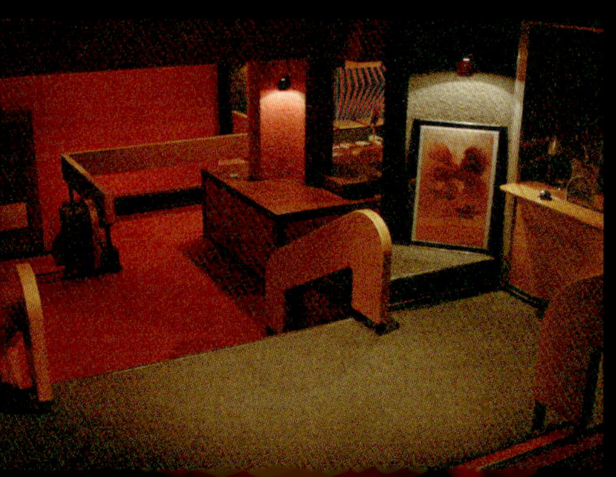

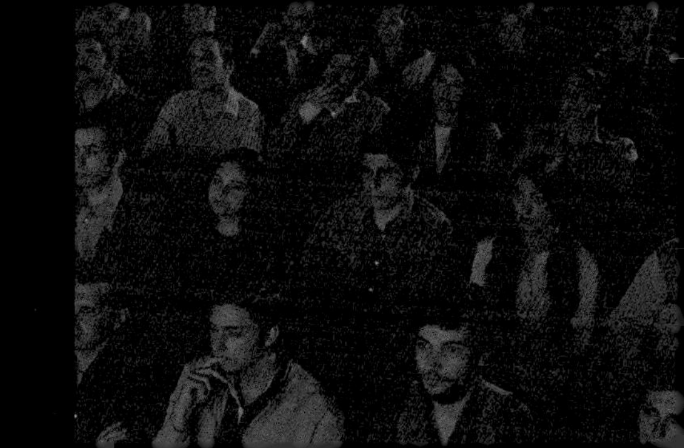

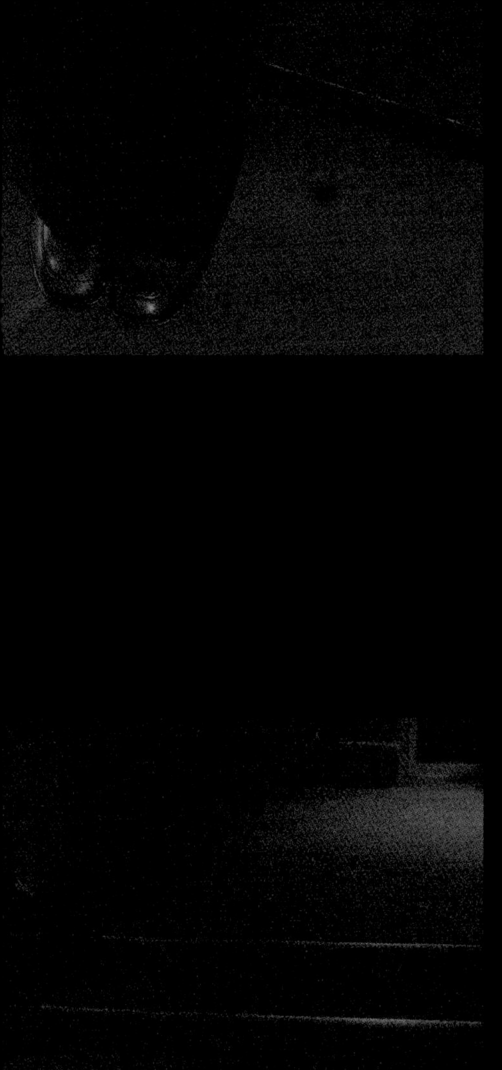

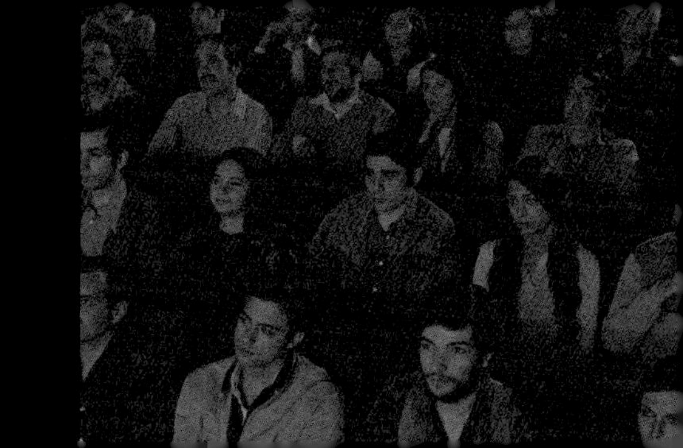

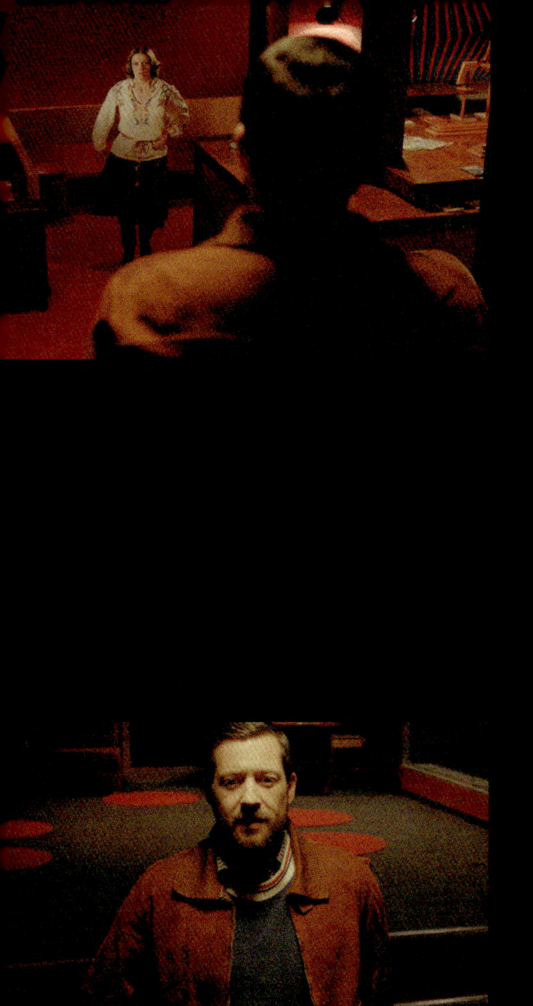

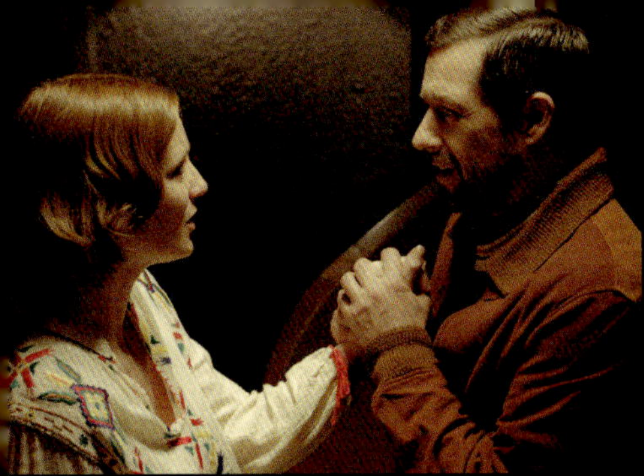

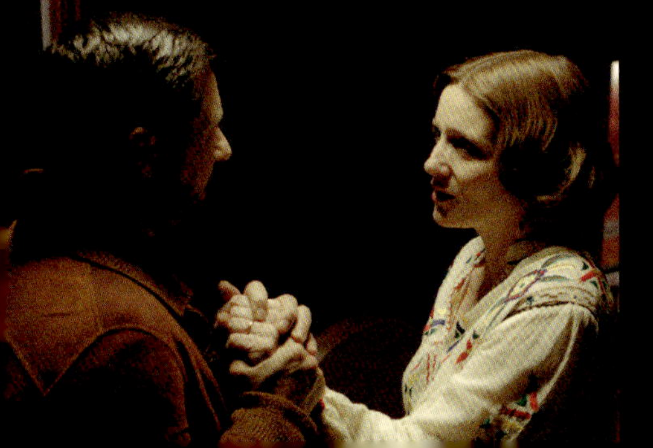

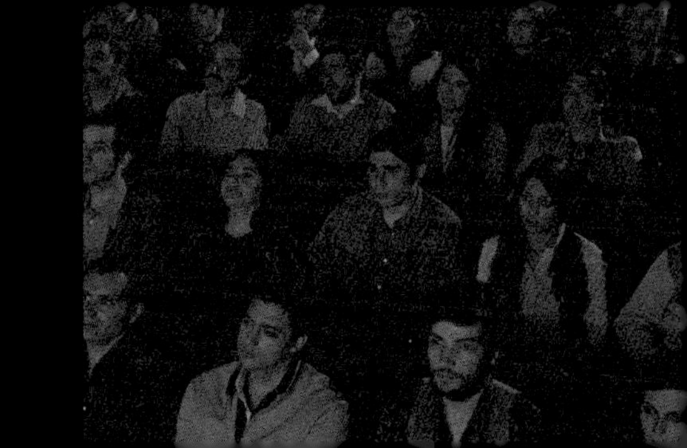

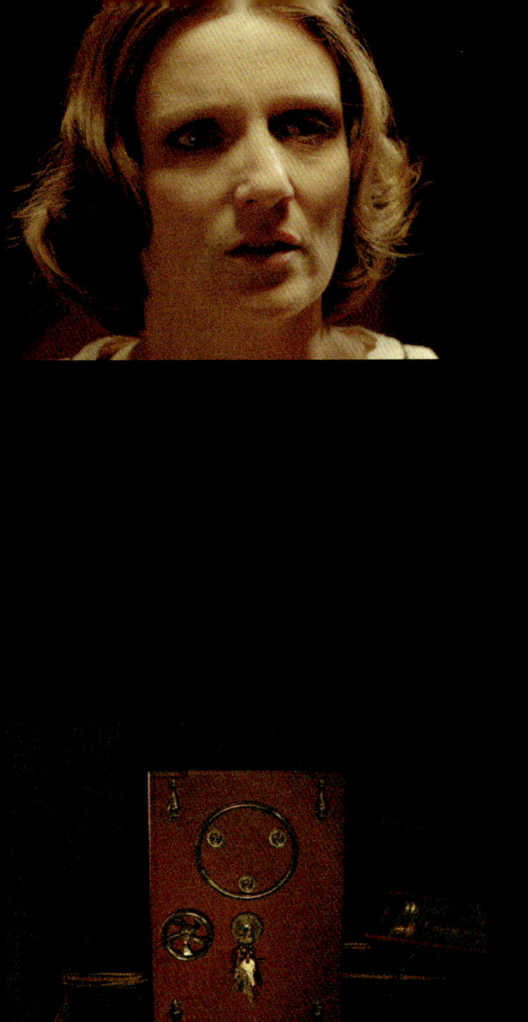

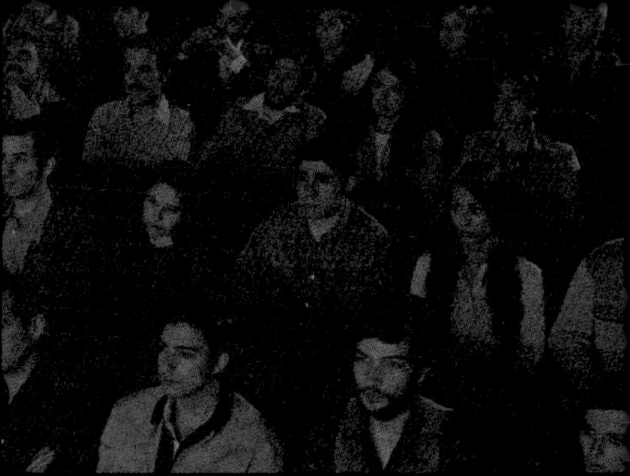

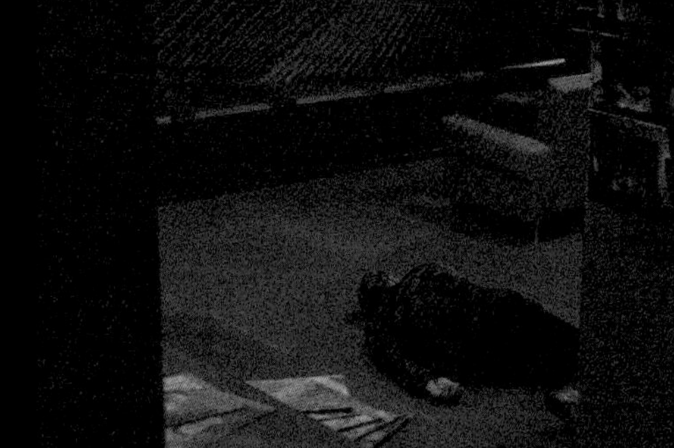

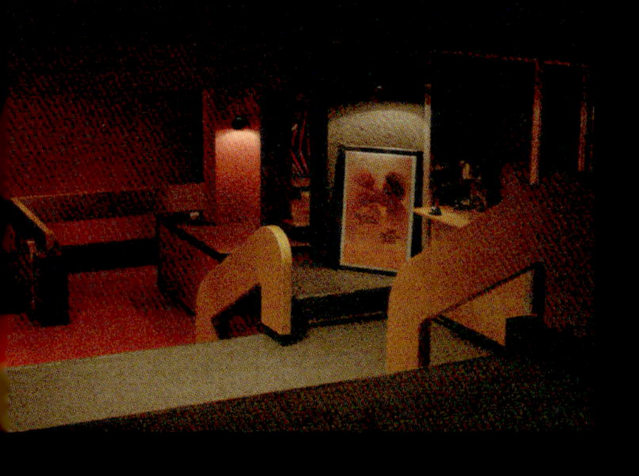

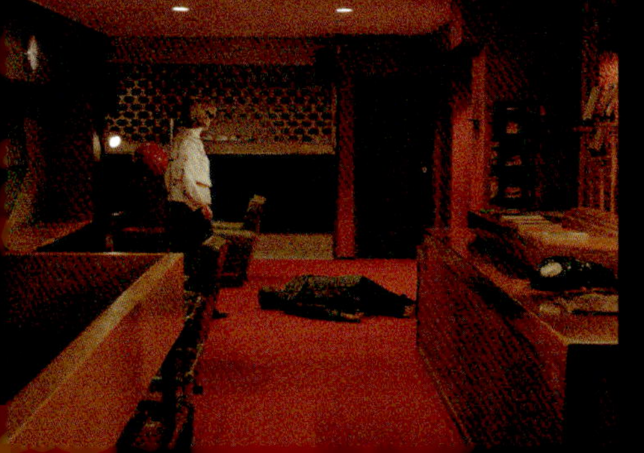

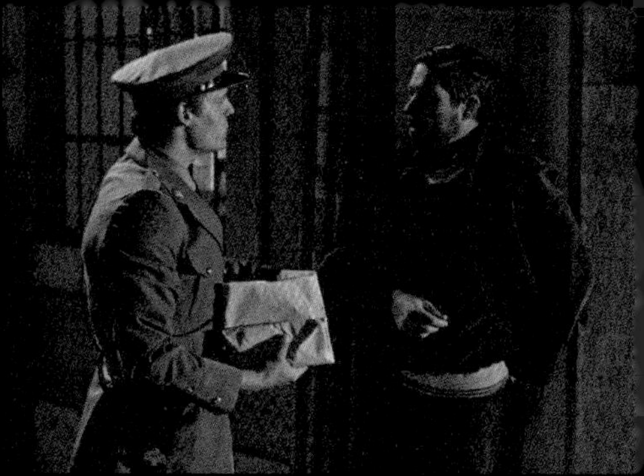

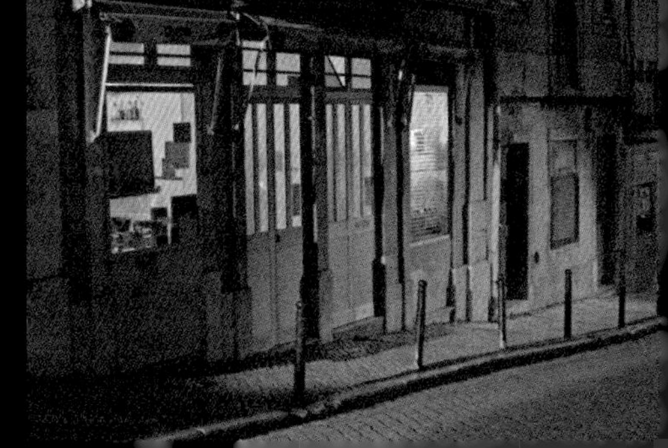

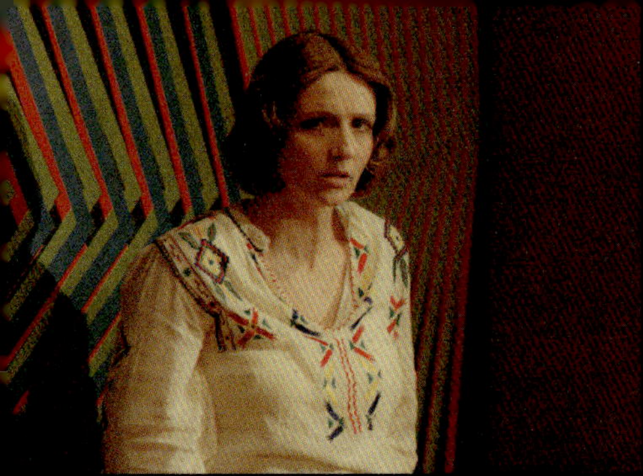

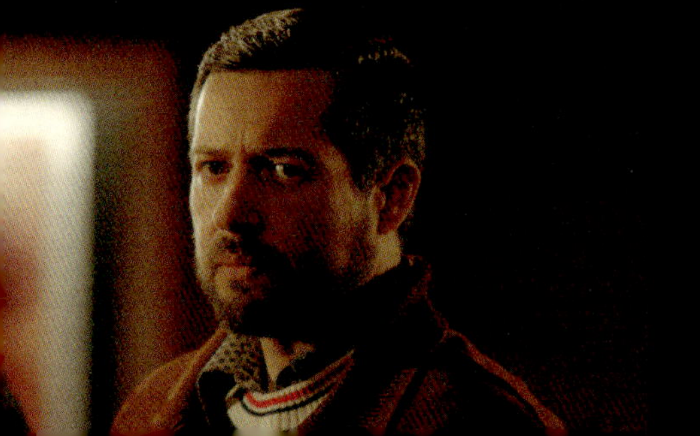

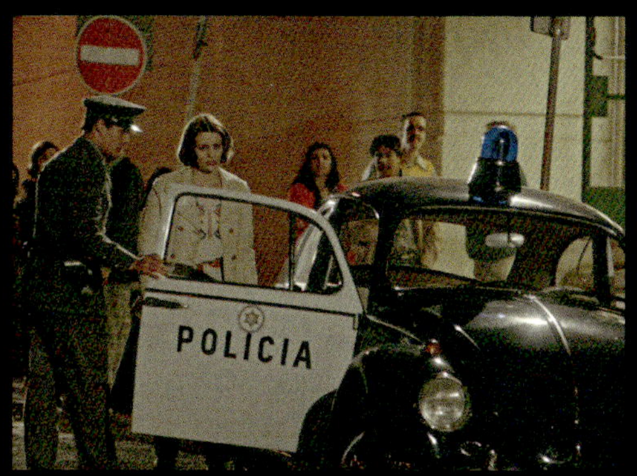

POLICIA

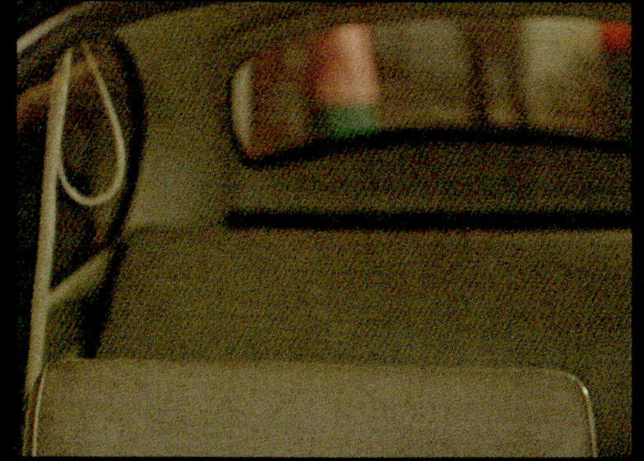

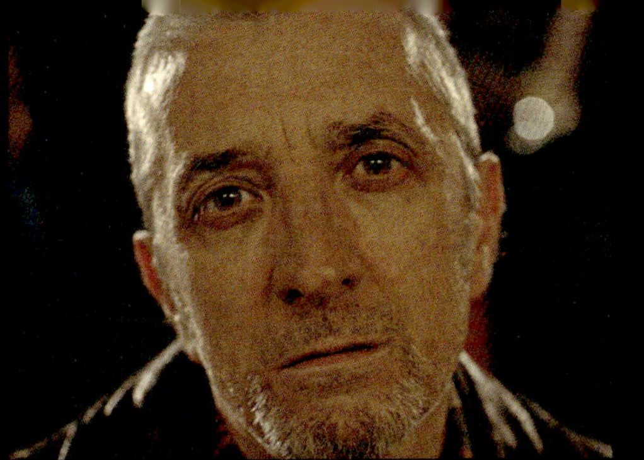

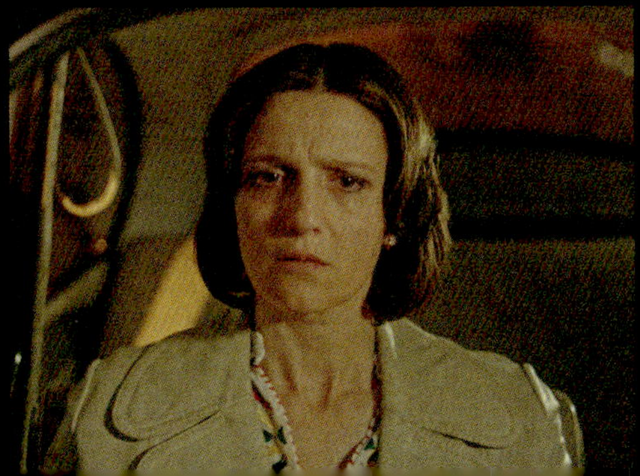

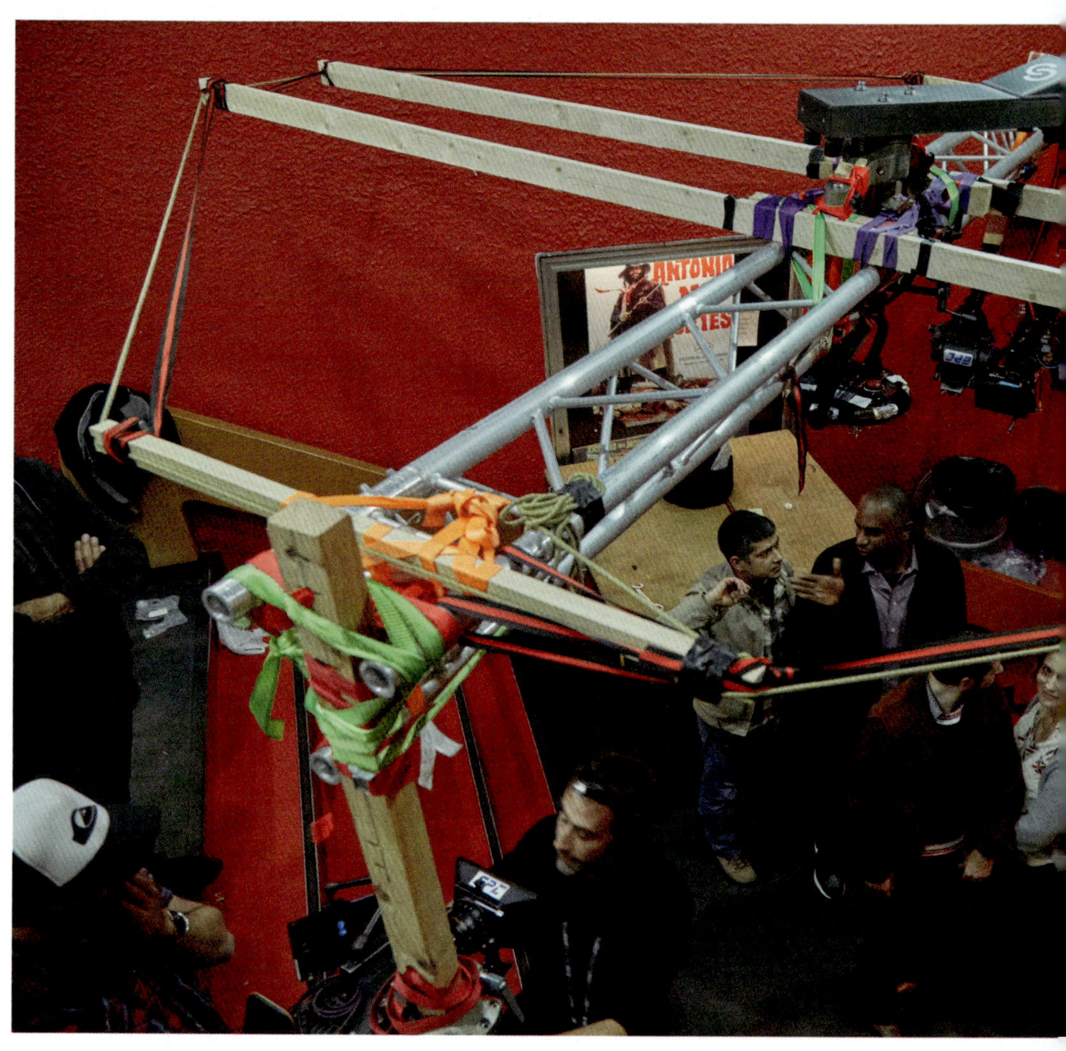

The Secret Agent, 2015
Production photographs by Yusuke Ito

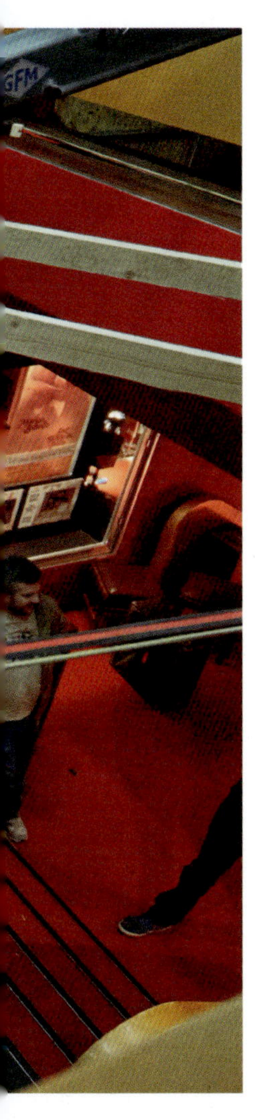

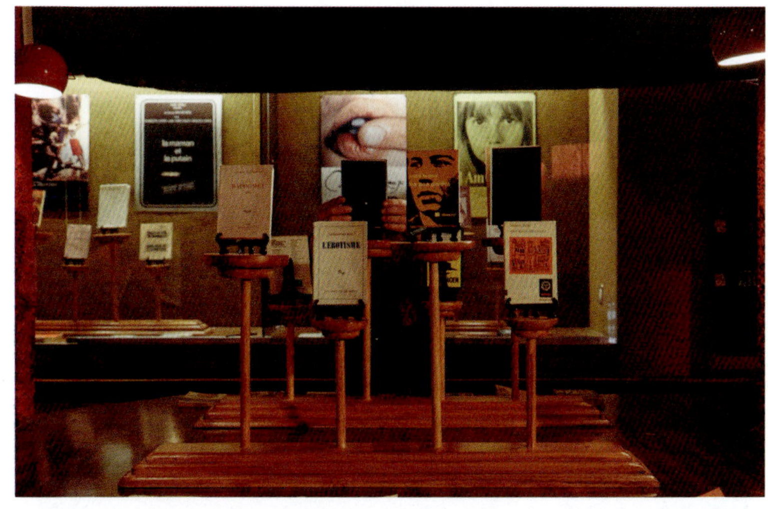

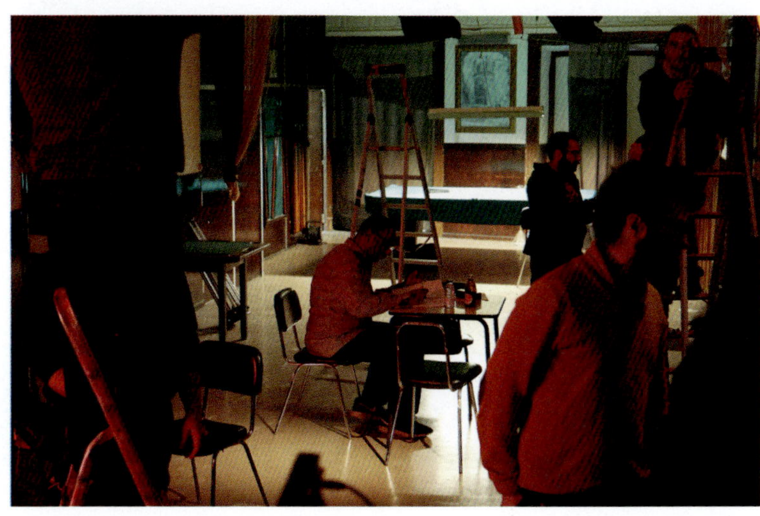

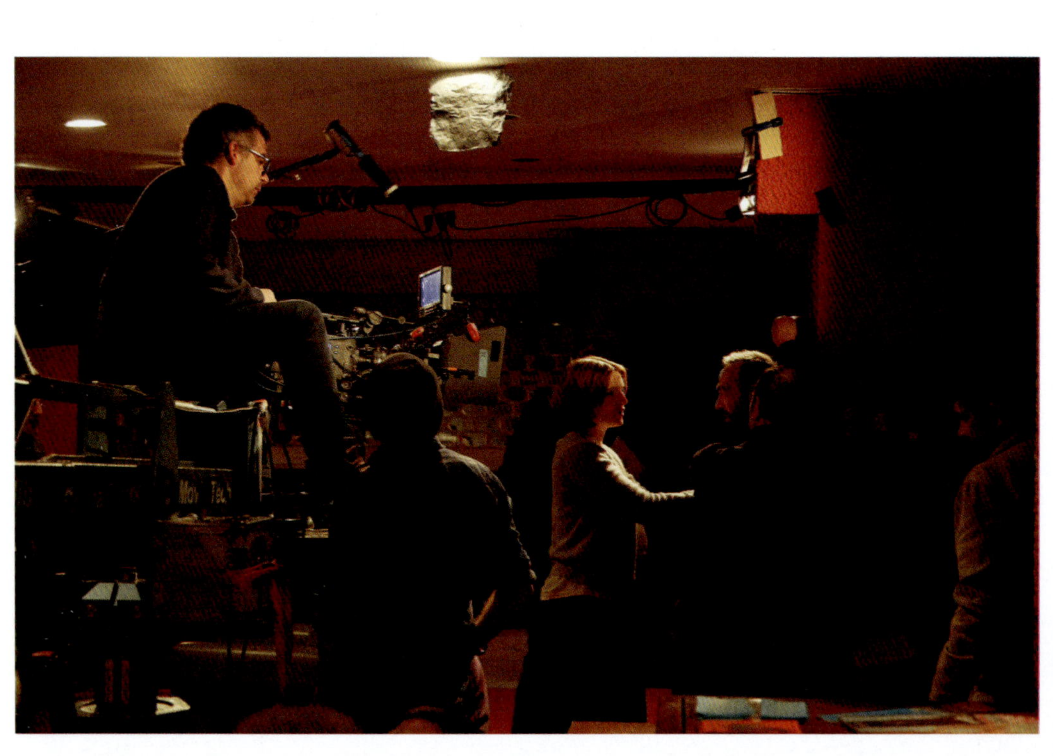

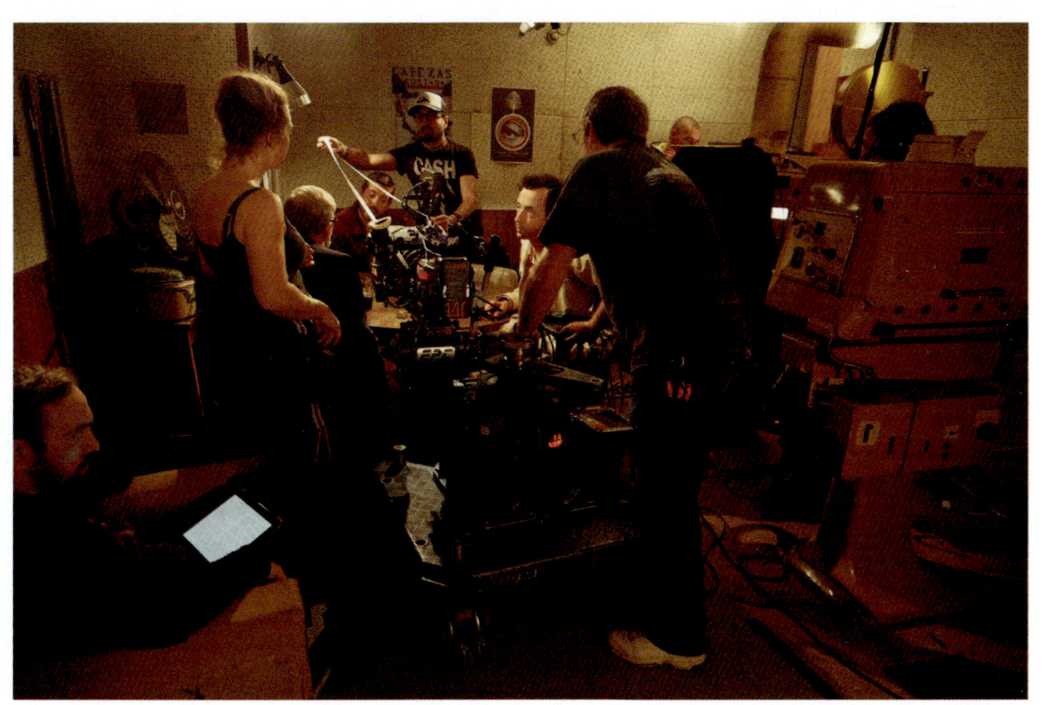

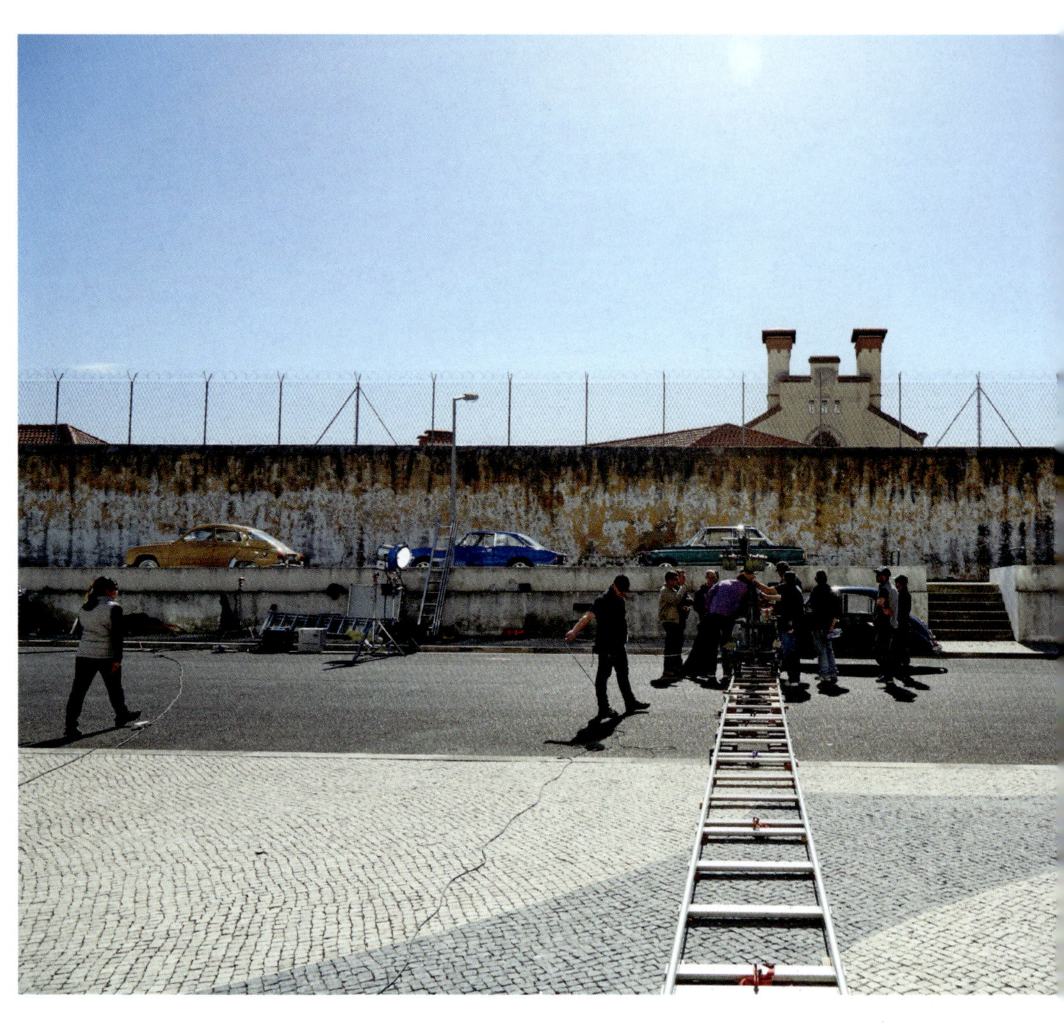

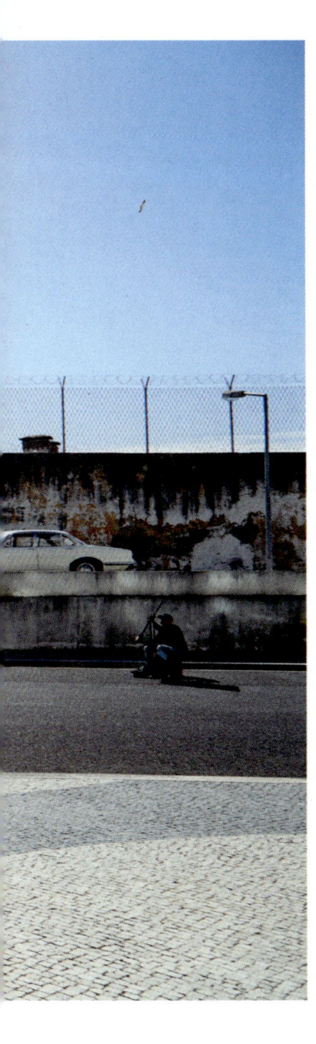

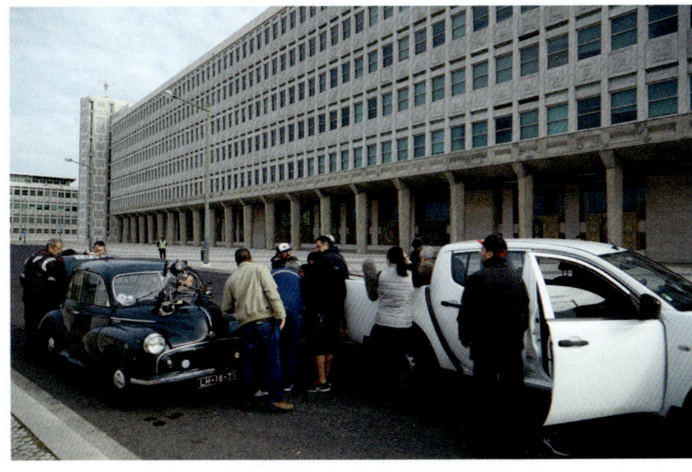

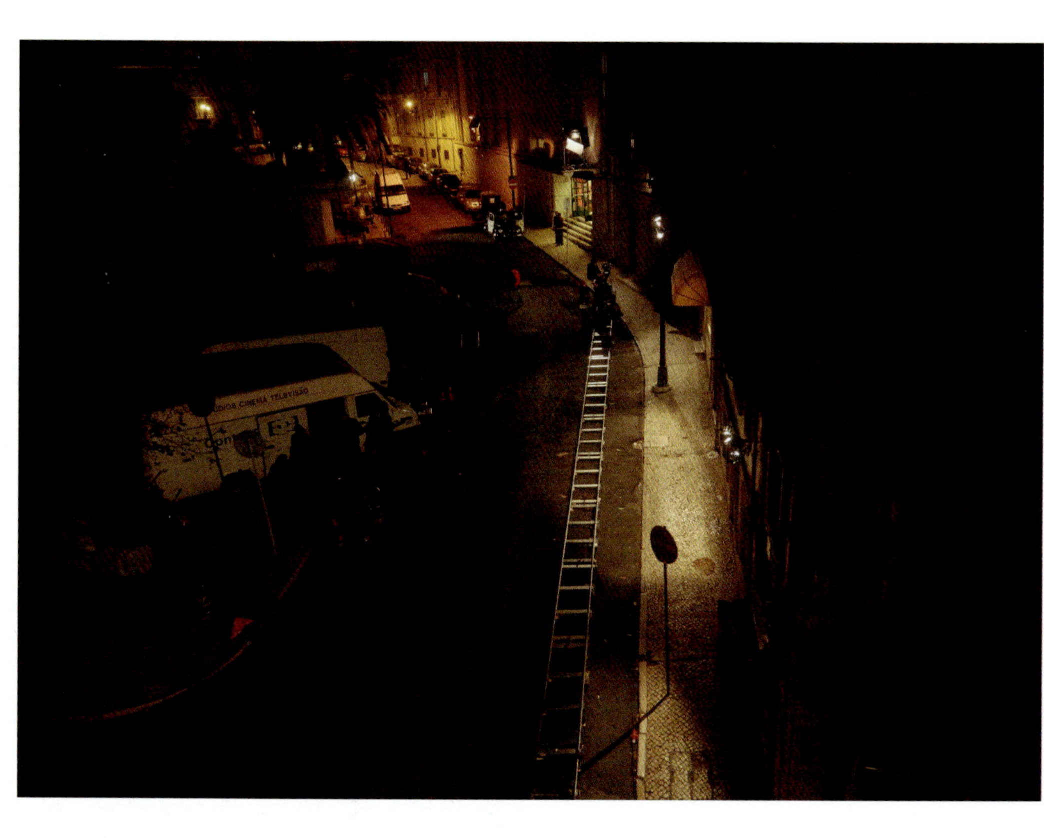

The Secret Agent

A SCRIPT BY STAN DOUGLAS
2015

CONTEXT

Joseph Conrad's *The Secret Agent* (1907) is a novel inspired by a failed terrorist bombing of the Greenwich Observatory in 1894. His protagonist, Mr Verloc, runs a pornographic bookshop in London that also houses an apartment where he lives with his wife Winnie and her autistic brother Stevie. Verloc is the leader of an anarchist cell and, unbeknownst to his comrades, a spy in the employ of an unnamed but probably Russian Embassy. His Embassy handler tells he that if he wants to stay on the payroll he must orchestrate a "display of imbecile ferocity" and bomb the Observatory to terrify the middle class into docility. But Verloc has no confidence in his fellow travellers and makes use of his brother-in-law with tragic consequences.

Portugal was ruled by António Salazar's authoritarian "Estado Novo" regime from 1932 until it was overthrown by military coup on 25 April 1974. The left-leaning Armed Forces Movement (MFA) had wide popular support because of its opposition to unwinnable colonial wars and the revolution was relatively bloodless – until the months following a poll carried out to replace the fascist-era constitution. The Portuguese Communist Party was the oldest and most pervasive political organization in the country and poised to take power, but hostility toward its influence precipitated the so-called "Hot Summer" of 1975 during which numerous terrorist attacks were carried out by extreme left- and right-wing groups. Until a constitutional government was elected in 1976 the threat of instability was taken seriously by NATO, which began performing war games in the region, and by the United States, which ordered its battleships to keep watch off the coast.

This screenplay is based on Conrad's novel and set in Portugal ca. 1975.

DRAMATIS PERSONAE

LEADS

ALEXANDER VERLOC 40s, was born in Porto to British parents and speaks with an accent that betrays a posh education. Seven years ago, in the spring of 1968, he infiltrated French anarchist groups that he goaded into outlandish acts of sedition until being arrested. A citizen by birth, he fled to Portugal where he runs a movie theatre that allows him to discretely conduct his espionage.

WINNIE VERLOC 30s, is divorced and because of that estranged from her family. She occasionally has chilly conversations with her mother but that is only because her son STEVIE and his grandmother are close. Whenever VERLOC recounts his dreams they invariably end in the middle, but that is long after WINNIE has deduced that they are allegories of his secret business with the US Embassy.

MR VLADIMIR 40s, is an Embassy official whose predecessor was sacked for not anticipating the 1974 revolution. He finds himself burdened with informants whose connection to the "Estado Novo" regime makes them all but useless. He is particularly fed up with VERLOC who has not supplied decent intelligence in at least four years. Cruel.

INSPECTOR HEAT 40s, has because of his commitment to policing and indifference to politics been able to maintain the rank of Chief Investigator before and after the revolution. The cases he has been able to solve thanks to VERLOC's intelligence has made him a minor celebrity and this has gone to his head.

THE PROFESSOR 50s, is a nihilist who will explain his dark cosmology to anyone willing to listen. He feels safe from arrest because at any instant the binary chemical explosive he always carries on is person can destroy everything within a 20 meters radius but, until recently, that was in theory only.

THOMAS OSSIPON 30s, French, is a former student of medicine and pamphleteer of Maoist propaganda. He missed Mai 68 because he was vacationing at the time but has dropped out of medical school in order to travel to Portugal so he can witness a revolution first-hand.

PRINCIPALS

MICHAELIS 40s, is a former political prisoner who survives by providing provocative entertainment to left-leaning members of the aristocracy. He completely lacks empathy and speaks with a wild affect that his admirers mistake for wisdom.

KARL YUNDT 60s, is a former military officer relieved of duty for being politically suspect. He is a misanthrope who subscribes to no particular ideology and is amused by the suffering of others.

ASSISTANT COMMISSIONER 30s is a middle-ranking COPCON official and veteran of colonial wars. He is frustrated by HEAT'S smug insubordination but knows that the Inspector is too well respected to be fired without good reason.

SECRETARY OF STATE OF JUSTICE 40s, is a Stalinist recently appointed to this post in spite of a lack of relevant experience. He regards politics not as ideological conflict but as sport and intends to be a champion.

EMBASSY FUNCTIONARY 20s, received his PhD in International Law at an astonishingly early age. Rude.

TITLE: TWO WEEKS EARLIER

INT. EMBASSY CORRIDOR — DAWN.

The FUNCTIONARY leads VERLOC down a corridor
in the Ornate Embassy Building.

> FUNCTIONARY
>
> You're late.

> VERLOC
>
> The buses don't run this early and I don't
> have a car.

> FUNCTIONARY
>
> Well you should have rented one. You know
> Mr Vladimir doesn't like to be kept waiting.

> VERLOC
>
> What's this about?

> FUNCTIONARY
>
> We are not very satisfied with the competence
> of the Police. And the leniency of the Judicial
> Branch is pathetic. We need them to take
> charge of the situation.
> (Beat)
> I have read your reports. I wonder why you
> bothered to write them at all — are you aware
> that we read the local press?

> VERLOC
>
> I have recently uncovered some interesting
> facts. But I have not been able to verify them
> to my satisfaction.

                    FUNCTIONARY
                      (Ironic)
Really. The First Secretary will be very pleased.

At the door to MR VLADIMIR's office he knocks and
immediately enters.

INT. MR VLADIMIR'S OFFICE — DAWN.

MR VLADIMIR sits behind an enormous horseshoe-
shaped desk littered with papers. The FUNCTIONARY
places a bundle of papers in front of him.

                    VLADIMIR
Verloc?

                    FUNCTIONARY
                      (Nods)
Verloc.

He points to where VERLOC should stand then ignores
him on his way out. MR VLADIMIR begins reading and
lets VERLOC stand.

                    VLADIMIR
                     (Finally)
Seven years ago you incited French students
into acts of sedition. What did you get for that?

                    VERLOC
Nine months in La Santé.

                    VLADIMIR
That's not so much. Anyway it serves you right
for getting caught.

(Flipping more pages)
What have you got to say for yourself Mr Verloc?

VERLOC
I have nothing special to tell you. You
summoned me and here I am even though
it could have been dangerous for me –

VLADIMIR
Your comrades are a lazy bunch. Like you
they're rarely out of bed before noon. Don't
worry, next time I will come to you.
What are you supposed to be anyway?
Anarchist? Desperate communist?

VERLOC
Anarchist.

VLADIMIR
(Reading again)
So you began your connection with us by
inciting insurrection in France. You got
yourself arrested and have been here doing
nothing in particular for the last seven years.
Exactly why did my predecessor give
you cover?

VERLOC
I am Portuguese.

VLADIMIR
Are you?

VERLOC
I was born in Porto where my –

VLADIMIR

Never mind explaining. Six years ago a lot
of lazy people were running this organization
and people like you got the wrong idea of
what this Embassy is. I want to correct that
misapprehension right now by telling you what
it is not: this is not a philanthropic organization.

VERLOC

I fail to understand –

VLADIMIR
(Stands)
You understand me perfectly Mr Verloc.
And as far as I can tell you have done nothing
to earn your salary in the last four years.
Now that I am here you will have to earn
your money. No work, no pay.

VERLOC
(Defensive)
Several times I have prevented what might
have been –

VLADIMIR

Don't tell me about the old days. The evil is
with us now. We don't want prevention we
want a cure. You know there are elections
coming up –

VERLOC

I do read the papers.

VLADIMIR

Well Portugal must be brought into line. You will
agree with me that the middle classes are stupid –

                    VERLOC

They are.

                    VLADIMIR

They have no imagination. What we need
to do is to stimulate them with a really good
scare. What's the most important thing to
the Portuguese people Mr Verloc?

                    VERLOC

I would say –

                    VLADIMIR

You don't know because you are too lazy to
think. They don't care about royalty or religion,
the fascists drove the aristocrats into hiding and
the church is tainted along with the old regime.
See what I mean?

                    VERLOC

Perfectly. What about the embassies? A series
of bombings directed at –

                    VLADIMIR

Don't be facetious Mr Verloc. You could blow up
every Embassy in Lisbon without influencing
the public one bit. The only thing the Portuguese
care about now is the future. They never want
to be a backward country again. You anarchists
hate the status quo and since bombs are your
means of expression why not bomb modernity
itself?
                    (Dramatic pause)
What do you think about an assault on
communication?

VERLOC

Communication –

VLADIMIR

Blow up the Marconi installation at Sesimbra
Mr Verloc. Sever the umbilical between
Europe and the New World. All European
telecommunication with America would
be disrupted for months.

What makes Portugal a modern nation?
The colonies it couldn't afford? Its useless
industry? No it's that braid of copper under the
Atlantic Mr Verloc. Why do you think a gang
of fascists was welcomed by NATO for the last
twenty-five years?

Before the first free election in half a century
we want a strategy of tension that will make the
middle classes think twice before they vote.

VERLOC

A difficult proposition.

VLADIMIR

What's the matter? Don't you have your pathetic
cronies at hand? I see that old terrorist Yundt
almost everyday moping around Jardim da
Estrela. And Michaelis, that deranged prophet
of the Lusitanian doom, you don't expect me to
believe you don't know where he is. Because if
you don't I will tell you.

VERLOC

It would require a lot of money.

VLADIMIR

Fuck you Verloc. That won't fly. You'll get your

allowance and not a penny more until something
happens. And if nothing happens you won't get
even that.

INT. SILENUS BAR — DAY.

The PROFESSOR and OSSIPON sit in glorious squalor
of a club filled with decorations and furnishings that only
get replaced when they fall off the wall or into pieces.
The WAITER watches a pair of POOL PLAYERS as
PROFESSOR reads the latest issue of OSSIPON's paper —

                    PROFESSOR
                  (Putting it down)
        Farmers —

                    OSSIPON
        Exactly. Portugal is perfect because the major-
        ity of the people is proletarianized already.

                    PROFESSOR
                    (Chuckles)
        Proletarianized.
        You are beginning to think like me comrade —

                    OSSIPON
        Hardly.

                    PROFESSOR
        Are you planning on tilling the fields anytime
        soon?
            I didn't think so. In your fantasy you will be
        running the show. The only difference between
        you and me is that I am proud to admit that I am
        better than everyone else.

OSSIPON
I swear sometimes you drive me mad.

Long pause. PROFESSOR looks at him. OSSIPON
shrugs, "Quoi?" PROFESSOR points at his empty glass.
OSSIPON snaps his fingers to get the waiter's attention.

PROFESSOR
There is no such thing as madness anymore.
The world is mediocre, limp, without force.
Force is a crime in the eyes of the weak who
rule us. Give me madness and I will move
the world. Ossipon, you will only ever have
my disdain because you can not even imagine
what the average person would call a crime.

BARTENDER arrives and deposits the next round.
Longer pause. PROFESSOR drinks as OSSIPON sulks.
Finally —

PROFESSOR (CONT'D)
Why do you sit with me?

OSSIPON
I thought it was you who were sitting with me.

INT. CINEMA LOBBY — NIGHT.

Crossing the lobby WINNIE notices that the wall clock
reports 3:15, which is not right. She knocks on it but
the minute hand refuses to move. She heads for the
box office and, once inside, turns to find MICHAELIS
at the window. He accepts a ticket without a word
then drifts away.

INT. CINEMA — NIGHT — CONTINUOUS.

MICHAELIS takes a seat looks around to see if he's been noticed then, instead of heading for the projection booth, begins to watch the movie.

INT. BOX OFFICE LANDING — NIGHT — CONTINUOUS.

YUNDT has arrived.

>   YUNDT
>   (Slaps the counter)
>   Ticket.

>   WINNIE
>   (Repulsed)
>   Mr Yundt.

She tosses him a ticket. He heads off.

INT. CINEMA — NIGHT — CONTINUOUS.

YUNDT takes a seat watches the film for a moment as per protocol, then creeps toward to the projection booth failing to notice that MICHAELIS had been watching the film only a few places away, engrossed, weeping.

INT. BOX OFFICE LANDING — NIGHT — CONTINUOUS.

>   OSSIPON
>   (Charming)
>   Mrs Verloc.

>   WINNIE
>   Mr Ossipon.

She tears a ticket from the pad and slides it out the box office window. She recoils when he cradles her hand in his. He shakes off his disappointment and retreats to the cinema where he makes no pretence of watching the film and heads straight for the projection booth.

INT. PROJECTION BOOTH — NIGHT — CONTINUOUS.

VERLOC rewinds a reel of film as *Last Tango in Paris* unspools on a projector – and is projected upside down inside the booth. Enter YUNDT –

> VERLOC
> (Nods)

Karl.

> YUNDT
> (Sarcastically)

Comrade.

He makes for a small table with four chairs around it, pours himself a glass from the half-empty bottle of wine and lights a smoke.

> YUNDT
> (Turns to Verloc)
> So. What's this all about?

> VERLOC
> Let's just wait 'till everyone gets here shall we?

> YUNDT
> (On Ossipon's entry a while later)
> How's our French tourist this evening?

OSSIPON
(Ignoring that)
Where is Michaelis? He's usually the first
one here.

VERLOC
I have no idea. I always tell him to arrive an
hour early.

YUNDT
Probably dining with his aristocrat.

OSSIPON
(Helping himself to wine)
I can't believe his luck. All he has to do is write
his memoirs and she pays all the bills.

YUNDT
He is a parasite feeding off another kind of
parasite.

OSSIPON
Don't you have a woman looking after you?

YUNDT
I have a wife: she is devoted to me. Aristocrats
need to be taken to the gallows not the classroom.

OSSIPON
Educating them won't hurt. Scientifically
speaking, what really matters is the mood of the
people. They need to have the impression that
the Revolution is moving in the right direction.
They're skittish and violence now is not the
answer.

YUNDT
(Pounding the table)
Violence is always the answer. It is the
only thing the masses understand — if they
understand anything at all.

OSSIPON

Which is why we need to be careful. They're in an
anxious mood but it will turn around in the end.

YUNDT

In the end we are all dead. Do you know what
I would call the present state of the Revolution?
Cannibalism. It's degenerated into the kind of
corruption you can find anywhere. The army
keeps the population at bay while deals are
brokered in back rooms.

Watching this spectacle leads VERLOC to the conclusion
that his gang will never be able to effectively collaborate
on anything.

OSSIPON

"They are playing a game. They are playing at
not playing a game. If I show them I see they
are, I shall break the rules and they will punish
me. I must play their game, of not seeing I see
the game."

YUNDT
(Recognizes the quote)
RD Laing is an ass. Michaelis raves about him
too. More relativist bullshit his mistress is feeding
him. Like all relativists he refuses to take a
position. He wants to be on everybody's side.
	I take my own side. How can you indulge
Michaelis in his ridiculous prophecies?

OSSIPON

You're a just bitter old man. You could never
understand that —

MICHAELIS
(Entering)

Sorry. I'm late.

VERLOC
(Annoyed)

You were supposed to be here an hour ago —

MICHAELIS

Sorry — the film is beautiful —
    Paul's loss reminds me of my own. It is a
loss we will all share —

YUNDT

More bourgeois bullshit. The film is ridiculous.
The Portuguese had been starved of such crap
for so long they line up all day to lap it up —

MICHAELIS

You don't understand —

YUNDT

You don't understand anything. People
are cattle —

OSSIPON
(Interrupting)

There's work to do. We'll finish this later —

VERLOC
(Angry)

Much later.

                    OSSIPON
You're in a filthy mood Alex.

                    VERLOC
Meeting's adjourned.

EXT. STREET — DAY.

SOLDIERS 1 & 2 lead PERPETRATOR to a military
vehicle. HEAT supervises, then watches it pull away to
reveal PROFESSOR sitting in a chair: he smiles, baring
rotten teeth. They approach one another and meet in
the middle of the street.

                    HEAT
Well?

                    PROFESSOR
Why don't you arrest me now? Fine
opportunity.

                    HEAT
I am not looking for you. When I want you
I know where to find you.

                    PROFESSOR
No doubt the papers would give you a glowing
obituary but if you lay your hands on me they
will have to bury us in the same grave.

                    HEAT
You couldn't frighten a child with your fairy
tales —

PROFESSOR

For a man of conviction this is a fine time for
self-sacrifice. You may not find another so
humane. The street's empty, there isn't even
a cat lounging around. You will never get me
at such a low cost of life and property —

HEAT
(Frustrated)
Give it up. Whatever it is you are doing. There
are simply too many of us for you.
(Professor smiles.)
Is something funny?

PROFESSOR
I am better at my work than you are at yours.

HEAT
(Walking away)
Fucking lunatic!

INT. CINEMA LOBBY — DAY.

VLADIMIR enters and rings the bell at the box office.

VERLOC
(Off)
Be with you in a minute.

He descends to the lobby and takes stock of the room.
Posters for films such as *I am Curious (Yellow)* and *Last
Tango in Paris* decorate the walls, surrealist and revolutionary literature is for sale. MR VLADIMIR passes
judgement as he waits. A while later VERLOC enters and
is surprised to find his Embassy handler standing there —

VLADIMIR

This is how you greet customers?

VERLOC

How would I know it was you sir?

VLADIMIR

Exactly. You must have thought it was
a customer. You should have hurried out
instead of yelling from the back room.

VERLOC

I came right out.

VLADIMIR

I had time to look at your inventory: revolutionary
literature by day obscene movies by night.
Intellectual pornography and the other kind.

VERLOC

Permit me to observe it's not very wise of you to
come here like this. It may destroy my usefulness.
If someone saw you – even my wife –

VLADIMIR

Your what?

VERLOC

My wife. I'm married.

VLADIMIR

Anarchists don't marry. They can't. It would
be apostasy. Where is she now?

VERLOC

Dropping off her son at my mother-in-law's.
She could be back at any moment.

VLADIMIR

He has a mother-in-law too. Don't you think
you're overdoing it bit? It's your own business —

VERLOC

It is my own business —

VLADIMIR

— but don't forget when you cease to be useful
you will cease to be employed.
            (Proffers a slip of paper)
We have ascertained the location for the event.
A spot where the cables come close to the
surface before they go to the ocean: Sesimbra.

VERLOC
            (Accepting it)
Of course.

VLADIMIR
            (Standing)
We're finished. Check and make sure none of
your friends are lurking outside.

VERLOC

Nobody comes by until the evening, if at all.
            (The front door scrapes open, he looks)
Damn. It's my wife.
            (Hands Vladimir a book)
Take this and act like a customer.

VLADIMIR

Don't forget Mr Verloc if nothing happens you
get nothing, except maybe the wrath of your
mother-in-law —
            (He exits, passing Winnie on the stair)

WINNIE
(Entering the lobby)
Who was that?

VERLOC

A client –

WINNIE

Must be new one. He was dressed like a
foreigner. What did he want?

VERLOC

A lot of things.
(A beat)
I may have to go on a short trip.

WINNIE

He's not one of those Embassy people who've
been bothering you lately?

VERLOC

Embassy people? Who has been talking to
you about Embassy people?

WINNIE

You have. In your sleep.
Who was he?

VERLOC

A businessman.

WINNIE
(Approaching)
So what about Sesimbra?

VERLOC
(Surprised)
Sesimbra?

WINNIE
You said that you would ask Michaelis to take
Stevie on little vacation there — at the cabin that
woman gave him.

VERLOC
(Relieved)
Right. I forgot. That's a good idea.

BLACK.

TITLE: TWO WEEKS LATER.

INT. SILENUS BAR — DAY.

A pair of MUSICIANS rehearses on a small stage, accompanied by a drum machine. The PROFESSOR sits alone
with a half-empty glass of beer in front of him. OSSIPON
makes a beeline for his table —

OSSIPON
(Approaching)
Were you out early today Professor?

PROFESSOR
In bed 'till eleven.

OSSIPON
Did you walk all the way from Palma de Baixo?

PROFESSOR
No. Bus.

OSSIPON

Have you been here long?

PROFESSOR

About an hour —
                    (Suspicious)
What is this?

OSSIPON

Haven't you heard the news?
                    (Sits)
It's amazing that you of all people — Do you just
sell your stuff to anyone who asks for it?

PROFESSOR

I never refuse my stuff to anybody on principle —

OSSIPON

What if an undercover a cop came along and
asked to see your wares?

PROFESSOR

They don't dare come near me.

OSSIPON

And why's that?

PROFESSOR
                    (Tapping his chest)
Because they know full well that I never part
with the last handful of "my wares." Enough to
turn this place to rubble.

OSSIPON

So I've heard.

                    PROFESSOR
And they have too. The pay is simply not good
enough for them to deal with a man like me.
And when I walk in a crowd I never let go
of this —
          (A pneumatic trigger in his hand)
One squeeze actuates the detonator.

                    OSSIPON
Instantaneous of course.

                    PROFESSOR
Sorry to say it isn't. Exactly four seconds elapse
between actuation and explosion.

                    OSSIPON
Four seconds? I would go mad.

                    PROFESSOR
Wouldn't matter if you did. Even the fastest
sprinter couldn't escape. In the end it's character
alone that guarantees one's safety. I have the
means to make myself deadly but that in itself
is no protection. What matters is that people
believe I have the will to use those means.

                    OSSIPON
And there is no one of character among the
people or the police?

                    PROFESSOR
They are all my inferiors because their character
is based on conventional morality and obedience
to the law. I stand apart from everything artificial.
They depend upon the social order, which, as
we saw recently, is complex and open to attack.

I on the other hand depend on death, which is
simple and cannot be attacked. My superiority
is self-evident.

                    OSSIPON
That's a pretty transcendental way of looking
at it. But I have heard Yundt say pretty much
the same thing —

                    PROFESSOR
Yundt has been a posturing clown his entire life.
The trouble with you and your gang is that you
can no more think independently than a journalist
or a grocer. You have no character whatsoever.
You and your politics.

                    OSSIPON
Then what you are after?

                    PROFESSOR
A perfect detonator.
     Don't make that face.

                    OSSIPON
I am not making a face.

                    PROFESSOR
You see? You can't even bear to hear anything
conclusive. You revolutionaries are slaves to
convention as much as the police. The police
play their little games and so do you. But I don't.
My experiments cost money and I occasionally
have to do without food for a day or two —
               (off Ossipon's look)
I have had two already and I'm about to
order another.

(Snaps his fingers at the waiter)
I'm having a little holiday.

OSSIPON
I'm afraid I'll have to spoil your little vacation:
a man was blown up at Sesimbra this morning.
(Consults his newspaper)
Not much so far, "Bombing on the coast...
foggy morning... enormous hole in the ground...
No doubt a wicked attempt to blow up Marconi..."
The rest is just the usual newspaper pap.
(To Professor)
My first thought was that you had solved that
"problem of scale" you were having.
(Professor nods)
This could effect our position very badly.
I can't believe you gave it away to the first idiot
who came along.

PROFESSOR
I would shovel my stuff into every corner of
every street if I had enough.

OSSIPON
Who was it? Can you describe the person you
sold it to?

PROFESSOR
I can describe him in a single word: Verloc.

OSSIPON
(Aghast)

Verloc?

PROFESSOR
I believe you know him. I understand he's the
leader of your group.

OSSIPON

Yes.
No —
Leader —
You don't know anything.
What was he was planning?

PROFESSOR

A demonstration against some building —

OSSIPON

What do you think happened?

PROFESSOR

I wouldn't know. Set the detonator and lost
track of the time —
On the other hand if catalysis was in progress
a sharp shock would set it off —
He either ran the time too close or let the
thing fall.

OSSIPON

Verloc. I saw him just last week. An intellectual
nonentity but he certainly had a talent for
working the police —
Did you know that he was married?

PROFESSOR

Who cares.

OSSIPON

She must have had some money for them to open
that place. He seemed to make it pay though.
Our problem now is how to disavow our
connection with that idiot —

PROFESSOR
You could ask the police. They know where
each one of you slept last night.

OSSIPON
Then they're aware we had nothing to do
with it – but what they tell the press is another
matter –
(Thinks)
Maybe I should bring Michaelis into town
and organize some kind of meeting. He spews
bullshit but it goes down well with a crowd.
      But I don't even know how to get in touch
with him –

PROFESSOR
He's on the coast writing a book. He imagines
a world that is like a gigantic hospital in which
everyone is injured and the strong devote
themselves to the nursing of the weak. I told
him I plan for a world where the weak are
taken in hand for extermination.

OSSIPON
And what remains?

PROFESSOR
I remain. If I am strong enough.

OSSIPON
That idiot Verloc –
      You made him blow himself to bits.

PROFESSOR
Not a bad death.

                    OSSIPON
I wonder what his wife will do now —
        (Snapping out of it)
Verloc left a real mess in my hands. Yundt's got
bronchitis and that will probably finish him.
Michaelis is away and never reads the paper —

                    PROFESSOR
He says they make him feel sad —

                    OSSIPON
And I'm short of cash at the moment.
        What am I going to do —

                    PROFESSOR
You already know what you're going to do:
you're going to ride the widow for all she's
worth.

INT. ASSISTANT COMMISSIONER'S OFFICE — DAY.

HEAT enters the ASS'T COMMISSIONER office, a plain
room lined with bookcases stocked with books that are
mostly ornamental.

                ASS'T COMMISSIONER
I didn't expect to see you back so soon.

                    HEAT
I was already out there when it happened.

                ASS'T COMMISSIONER
Did you identify the suspect?

                    HEAT
No. We had to remove him with a shovel. You
should have seen the coroner's face. The only

thing we could carry away intact were the legs stuffed into a pair of boots. The rest of him had to be scooped into a tarp. He must have tripped and it went off under his chest.

ASS'T COMMISSIONER
Person unknown, then.

HEAT
Persons, probably. A bus driver told me that in the past two weeks there were only two people who got off near Cabo Espichel that he didn't recognize: a man in his forties carrying a can of paint and another one about half his age. The younger man was fair-haired and that's about all he remembered, except that they both spoke English.

ASS'T COMMISSIONER
Foreigners.

HEAT
It is very frustrating to have outsiders interfering in our affairs.

ASS'T COMMISSIONER
(Annoyed)
Only a week ago I assured my superiors that all known anarchists were under observation and that no out-breaks of violence would occur before the election. You assured me that there wasn't one of them you couldn't lay your hands on at any moment. Now I have to tell —

HEAT
I am as angry as you are sir. I wish I were investigating a normal crime —

ASS'T COMMISSIONER
A normal crime?

HEAT
A crime committed by normal criminals. I can
understand what thieves and gamblers want
but these people – I don't think they themselves
know what they are after. It takes commitment
to be a thief but any idiot can be a terrorist from
one day to the next.

ASS'T COMMISSIONER
How about this –
(Consulting a file)
"Professor." A bomb-maker. Did he have
anything to do with this?

HEAT
It would be surprising.

ASS'T COMMISSIONER
What does that mean?

HEAT
I mean he is constantly watched.
We know his routine and we know that his
stuff doesn't work. I can tell you for a fact that
his group had nothing to do with this.

ASS'T COMMISSIONER
You're sure.

HEAT
I have a good idea of where each of them
slept last night.

ASS'T COMMISSIONER
So two men – one of whom is still at large –

HEAT
He's probably left the country by now –

ASS'T COMMISSIONER
(Getting worked up again)
– two men drop in from out of nowhere to cause
an outrage that seems to have no other purpose
than to create panic and make the Secretary of
State look like an idiot. There must be something else Inspector. I can't believe that your
morning at Sesimbra was completely wasted.

HEAT
Not completely.

ASS'T COMMISSIONER
Then how do you plan to proceed?

HEAT
By keeping an eye on Michaelis.

ASS'T COMMISSIONER
(Surprised)
Michaelis? No.

HEAT
He is a celebrity and a friend of the Secretary
but the evidence is hard to ignore.

ASS'T COMMISSIONER
You have evidence against Michaelis?

HEAT
It's just an intuition, really. He prophesizes
that the Revolution will be fulfilled in absolute
equality —

ASS'T COMMISSIONER
Sure. The people lap that stuff up —

HEAT
But have they thought through what he means
by "The Cleansing to Come"?

ASS'T COMMISSIONER
That's just a metaphor.

HEAT
Is it? The driver remembered the two men
getting off at Azeitão, which is in the middle
of nowhere but less than a half a kilometer from
Michaelis' cottage. He's supposedly writing
a book —

ASS'T COMMISSIONER
I've heard. Is there anything else?

HEAT
The body of a man blown to bits —

ASS'T COMMISSIONER
Don't be sarcastic with me Inspector.

HEAT
When I interviewed Michaelis he seemed to
be very nervous and I —

ASS'T COMMISSIONER
You're police and he was a prisoner for twenty
years —

HEAT
(Sits)
If there is some reason for not interfering with
Michaelis you should let me know.

ASS'T COMMISSIONER
That's not what I mean and you know it.
We both know how tenuous hearsay evidence
can be.

SECRETARY
(Knocks, then pokes her head in)
Sir?

ASS'T COMMISSIONER
What is it?

SECRETARY
From the coroner —

The ASS'T COMMISSIONER makes an affirmative
noise. She enters and hands him a manila envelope.
Once she has gone he slips the contents out onto
his desk —

ASS'T COMMISSIONER
I asked for photographs of all the evidence
to me as soon as he was done with it.
(A photograph)
Do you recognize this?

HEAT

That's the scene from this morning. I was there
when the picture was taken —

ASS'T COMMISSIONER
(Another photograph)

How about this?

HEAT

It looks like one of the bomber's boots —

ASS'T COMMISSIONER
(And another)

Correct. And this?

HEAT

I don't know sir.

ASS'T COMMISSIONER

An address: "Rua do Loreto, 12." What's at
Rua do Loreto, 12?

HEAT
(Deflated)

A cinema.

ASS'T COMMISSIONER

You been there?

HEAT

I know the man who runs it. He has been of use
to us more than once.

ASS'T COMMISSIONER

I've never heard of this place. Were any of my
predecessors aware of what you just told me?

HEAT

No sir. A man like that becomes useless once he loses his anonymity.

ASS'T COMMISSIONER

I see.

How did you come into contact with him?

HEAT

About seven years ago I was helping coordinate security for the US Embassy. One afternoon I was sent word that a visiting Senator wanted to see me personally. He invited me into his apartment where an Englishman was waiting for us. He had news that there would be an attempt on the Senator's life at the opera that evening. I turned my head for a moment to talk to the Senator and when I looked back the man was gone. Anyway I acted on his information and was able to avert what might have been a very ugly incident. A few months later I saw the man from the Embassy leaving Santa Apolónia Station and followed him to Rua do Loreto. But I suppose you are not interested in hearing in any of this —

ASS'T COMMISSIONER

Your business with this Embassy spy is all that interests me right now —

HEAT

I reminded him of our first encounter and he told me that he was settled down, married, and all he wanted was to be left alone. I promised that as long as he didn't get mixed up in anything outrageous the police would take no notice of him.

                    ASS'T COMMISSIONER
And what did he give you in exchange for your
protection?

                          HEAT
Whenever I had the feeling something was in the
air I would drop a note at his place and he would
respond the same way at mine. I always found he
could tell me something worth knowing.

                    ASS'T COMMISSIONER
He failed you this time.

                          HEAT
I had no idea anything was going to happen.
I asked him nothing so he told me nothing.
It's not like we were paying him.

                    ASS'T COMMISSIONER
No he's a secret agent in the employ of a foreign
government.
        What's his name?

                          HEAT
Alexander Verloc —

INT. CINEMA LOBBY — DAY.

VERLOC descends the staircase then enters the lobby —

                         WINNIE
You were supposed to open today —

                         VERLOC
Couldn't. Business.

WINNIE

There's *Cozido* on the stove —

VERLOC

I'm not hungry.

WINNIE

It's lonely here with Stevie away — where were you all day?

VERLOC

Lots of places. I went to the bank. I drew out money.

WINNIE

I didn't know we had to pay anything —

VERLOC

Well I drew it out.

WINNIE

What all of it?

VERLOC

Yes all of it.

WINNIE

What did you do that for?

VERLOC

To have it handy. We may need it.

WINNIE

What's going on?

VERLOC

You know you can trust me.

WINNIE

I wouldn't have married you if I didn't trust
you Mr Verloc.
	Alex —
	Why are you still standing there? You're
not going out again are you?

VERLOC

I've had enough of going out. What I want is
to go away for good. Get out of all this —

WINNIE

You have been talking about emigrating for
the past year but things are finally changing
here — We should at least wait until the fall.

VERLOC

I am sick of this life. I've had enough —

WINNIE

You don't have to work for those foreigners
any more. Nobody needs to do that anymore.
Business is good. We have a nice apartment.
You're not tired of me.

VERLOC

Of course not. Winnie —
		(The bell rings. He turns to see the
		Assistant Commissioner)
I may have to go out again —

WINNIE

You just got back.

                    VERLOC
     Have to – if he asks me to – business –

                    WINNIE
     Get rid of that man, whoever he is, and come
     back to me. Get it over with.
                    (Verloc turns to exit)
     Maybe you should leave it with me.

                    VERLOC
     What?

                    WINNIE
     The money.

                    VERLOC
     Right.

He hands it to her then ascends the stairs. She watches
him exit.

EXT. MINISTRY OF JUSTICE – DAY.

HEAT creeps along in his car, watching the
ASS'T COMMISSIONER walking in the building's
long colonnade. The ASS'T COMMISSIONER
stops and HEAT parks.

INT. MINISTRY OF JUSTICE – DAY.

                SECRETARY OF STATE
                 (Upon his entry)
     Where the hell have you been Captain?

ASS'T COMMISSIONER
(Approaching)
Collecting information. The incident is
becoming a little messy.

SECRETARY OF STATE
You think I don't know that? I'm knee-deep in
shit. Everyone wants to know what happened
and what I'm going to do about it and you have
left me waiting all afternoon.

ASS'T COMMISSIONER
There were a lot of things to do. First a debrief
from Chief Inspector Heat.

SECRETARY OF STATE
(Relieved)
Ah Heat. Good.

ASS'T COMMISSIONER
You may not be relieved for long sir.

SECRETARY OF STATE
What? Why not?

ASSISTANT COMMISSIONER
He was reporting to me on his investigation
and eventually said something that made me
concerned for your position –

SECRETARY OF STATE
Me? What have I got to do with any of this?

ASS'T COMMISSIONER
He tried to drag Michaelis into it.

SECRETARY OF STATE

No.

ASS'T COMMISSIONER

Yes. I realized that if Heat had his way Michaelis
might wind up in jail again which would be very
embarrassing to you given the way you have
been championing him as a victim of the old
regime —

SECRETARY OF STATE

This isn't happening —

ASS'T COMMISSIONER

Heat and I fenced for a while, until I received
an interesting photograph from the coroner:
of a boot with an address inside it. The address
of an Embassy operative.

SECRETARY OF STATE

A what?

ASS'T COMMISSIONER

I know sir. We have been spending the past
year trying to rid ourselves of spies and informants and they continue to crop up. His name is
Alexander Verloc and he has been in touch with
Heat for at least seven years — It's funny to think
that the reputation of the great Inspector Heat
might all be the work of an obscure Embassy spy.

SECRETARY OF STATE

You have him in custody?

ASS'T COMMISSIONER

Heat?

SECRETARY OF STATE
No, the other. We'll make an example of
Heat later.

ASS'T COMMISSIONER
I just came from a long conversation with him.
When I told him I wanted to talk about Sesimbra
he went pale. He claimed it was an accident and
I believed him. I believed that he didn't expect
anyone to die anyway —

SECRETARY OF STATE
You brought him in?

ASS'T COMMISSIONER
Not yet. I told him to go home and put his affairs
in order. I don't think there's any chance of flight.
The Embassy will hunt him down if he flees
and his comrades will kill him if they find out he
has been working under a false flag. He knows
prison will be the safest place for him while we
prepare our case against Mr Vladimir —

SECRETARY OF STATE
We'll arrest the spy tomorrow and detain
Vladimir before he gets wind of anything — the
sanctimonious prick. Despite the way he
behaves he is just an Embassy employee and
has no immunity.
        There will be a trial —
                (Stands. Oratorial)
There will be a trial with startling disclo-
sures — that an employee of the Embassy was
behind a horrible and senseless attack upon the
people of Portugal.

(To ass't commissioner)
This will be good for us both Captain.

INT. CINEMA LOBBY — NIGHT.

HEAT descends the staircase as EMPLOYEE and
USHER exit the lobby.

                    WINNIE
See you tomorrow Pedro —

                    EMPLOYEE
See you tomorrow Mrs Verloc —

WINNIE closes the grate on the CONCESSION STAND,
turns and HEAT is suddenly there.

                    HEAT
Good evening.

                    WINNIE
Evening.

                    HEAT
Is your husband in Mrs Verloc?

                    WINNIE
He's out. Who are you? I haven't seen you
before have I?

                    HEAT
I really wouldn't know but I remember seeing
you. Your husband and I had business together.

                    WINNIE
Well he's out.

                          HEAT
It's urgent Mrs Verloc. I could wait if you were
sure he wouldn't be long.

                          WINNIE
He never tells me.

                          HEAT
And you have no idea where he's gone.

                          WINNIE
No idea.

                          HEAT
But you know who I am —

                          WINNIE
I do?

                          HEAT
You know very well that I am police.
     My name is Heat. Chief Inspector Heat of
the Judicial Police. I want a little information.

                          WINNIE
Alex isn't here —

                          HEAT
And you don't know anything?

                          WINNIE
About what?

                          HEAT
I think you might have a pretty good idea of
what's going on if you tried.

WINNIE

What's going on?

HEAT

Don't you read the papers?

WINNIE

Not today. I was busy. What are they saying?

HEAT

Lots about an attempt to destroy the Marconi
Communications Centre with a bomb. Your
husband didn't mention it when he came home?

WINNIE

No.

HEAT

There is another small matter I would have
spoken to your husband about if he were in but
you will do. We came across what we believe is
a stolen boot.

WINNIE

We haven't lost a boot.

HEAT

That's funny we found one with your address
inside it.

WINNIE

Oh. That must be my son's boot —

HEAT

Is he around? Could I speak with him for a
moment?

WINNIE

No. He isn't here.

HEAT

But he lives with you.

WINNIE

He's gone on vacation. He's staying with a
friend of the family —

HEAT

Who's that friend of yours? What's his name?

WINNIE
(It starts to sink in)

Michaelis —

HEAT

OK. And your son, what does he look like
short and stocky?

WINNIE

Stevie's tall and slim —

HEAT

Is he sickly, prone to fits?

WINNIE

Who are you talking about?

HEAT

Your son.

WINNIE
(Confused)

He's fine —

HEAT
(Revealing the photograph)
Then why the label?

WINNIE
It was my mother's gift. She's always done that.
Why is it burnt —

VERLOC
(Entering)
You. What are you doing here?

HEAT
We need to talk Mr Verloc.

VERLOC
About what?

HEAT
About what.
(Dragging Verloc out of earshot)
About you. About two men and a can of paint —

INT. BOX OFFICE LANDING — NIGHT — CONTINUOUS.

HEAT
You are the other man aren't you? Are you
insane getting involved in something like that?

VERLOC
I had no choice. But now it's over now.
Everything will come out and they'll all
get burned.

HEAT
Remember if you give yourself away in this

game you will be knifed in the street by one
of your friends before the month is out.

                    VERLOC
Jail is the safest place for me now. I was
promised a light sentence, a year or two.

                    HEAT
Listen. I know who you were with this afternoon
and I can tell you from experience that he can
not be trusted. Get out now. Your friends all
think you're dead.

                    VERLOC
They do?

                    HEAT
Of course they do. The papers have reported
that there was only one bomber.

                    VERLOC
Really. How did you find me?

                    HEAT
        (Flashes the photograph. Verloc pales)
No one could have identified the body we had to
scrape it up with a shovel.

                    VERLOC
Not so fucking loud.

                    HEAT
        (Beat)
The best thing to do would be to slip away while
your comrades think you're dead. You have my
word that none of us will try to stop you.

VERLOC
What about the Commissioner?

HEAT
The Assistant Commissioner will have no
evidence if you are gone, and he will look like
an idiot for meddling in my investigation.

VERLOC
(Grave)
I can't run. I'm married Mr Heat.

HEAT
Alright.
     I better be going then.
     But you should know that I have docu-
mented each of your tips in such a way that it
looks as if I arrived at the intelligence independently. Try to drag me into this it will be
your word against mine.
               (He exits)

INT. CINEMA LOBBY — NIGHT — CONTINUOUS.

VERLOC returns to the lobby to find WINNIE flopped
in a chair, devastated.

VERLOC
Winnie. Winnie I'm sorry you had to find out
like that.
     I've been sick thinking about how to break
it to you.
     It was an accident. It wasn't supposed to
be this way. I must have told Stevie twenty
times how to handle the package. He must
have tripped. Stevie should be here with us
right now.

How do you think I feel?

Listen. We have to think about tomorrow.
You're going to have to have your wits about
you because I will be taken in the morning. I'll be
gone for a year maybe more. For my own safety.
But you've got to be strong. You know you could
have lost me too —

WINNIE

You murdered my son.

VERLOC

I? No. It was an accident. As much an accident
as if he had been hit by a car while crossing the
street. Do you think I'm a murderer? Do you
think I wanted the boy to blow himself up?
I was fond of him too. I have told you the truth.
What more do you want?

WINNIE
(Stands)

I want to die.

VERLOC
(Over her shoulder)

No you don't. You've got me. But we must talk
about the future. For a little while you are going to
have to manage things on your own for a year or
so, but they will let me out quietly and we will slip
away together. You will stand by me won't you?

Won't you say something?
(Comes around to face her)

What is going on in your head? I don't even
know how much you know.

WINNIE
They had to scrape him up with a shovel.

VERLOC
Damn.
        If I didn't know that you loved –
        I could have just disappeared right away.
They all think I'm the one blown to pieces.
Not your son.

WINNIE pushes VERLOC away from her with
increasing violence.

WINNIE
Yes, my son! My son was blown to pieces!
            (A push with every sentence)
Stevie was my son. You never treated like
your own.
                (Grabbing his face)
I loved him. I loved Stevie.
With last phrase she shoves him against the wall –
forcing a shelving bracket through the base of his skull.

The room was still but she hears a ticking. She looks
at the wall clock she knows is broken – still 3:15 – back
to VERLOC then to the floor below his dangling feet:
blood dripping at regular intervals producing the
"ticking" sound. The bell rings and she dries her eyes
with the back of a hand –

WINNIE (CONT'D)
Coming!

                    OSSIPON
Mrs Verloc.

                    WINNIE
    (The last person she wants to see right now)
Ossipon —

                    OSSIPON
Mrs Verloc have you been crying?

                    WINNIE
Why are you here?

                    OSSIPON
I came to see you. I haven't been able to stop
thinking about you. I wanted to see if I could
help you in your time of trouble.

                    WINNIE
My trouble?

                    OSSIPON
Yes.

                    WINNIE
How could you know what my trouble is?

                    OSSIPON
I do. When I realized Verloc was gone I
immediately thought of you.

                    WINNIE
Will you help me Tom?

OSSIPON

Of course Winnie. I have always had feelings
for you but you were always so distant.

WINNIE

I was married.

OSSIPON

You loved him.

WINNIE

I did love him. I was an unmarried woman
with a son. With Stevie. Two helpless people.
Alex seemed to be a decent man. He wanted
me anyway. What was I supposed to do?

OSSIPON

You are free now. How did you find out about
the bombing?

WINNIE

From the police.

OSSIPON

The police!

WINNIE

Yes. Inspector Heat was here.

OSSIPON

Heat!

WINNIE

He pulled out a photo, "Do you recognize
this?" he said. Just like that.

OSSIPON

Heat himself! Here? What did he do?

WINNIE

Nothing. He went away.
    Just like the other one.

OSSIPON

Another inspector?

WINNIE

I don't know. He might have been one
of those Embassy people.

OSSIPON

Embassy. What are you saying? What
Embassy?

WINNIE

I don't know. What does it matter?

OSSIPON

What did he want?

WINNIE

I don't remember. Nothing. I don't care.
    Tom you've got to get me out of here!

OSSIPON

You mean now? This is all getting very
complicated.

WINNIE

Yes, now. We have to go away.

                         OSSIPON
Away? Where –

                         WINNIE
Away – To Rio – Anywhere.

                         OSSIPON
That's not a bad idea. The only problem
is I don't have a lot of money.

                         WINNIE
I have money. I have the money Tom.
Let's go now.

                         OSSIPON
How much money?

                         WINNIE
All the money.

                         OSSIPON
What do you mean all the money? All the
money Verloc had in the bank or what?

                         WINNIE
Yes. I've got it all.

                         OSSIPON
Already? How –

                         WINNIE
He gave it to me himself.

                         OSSIPON
                      (Confused)
OK. Well we'll be fine then.

                    WINNIE
Then let's go.

                    OSSIPON
Where's the money?

                    WINNIE
In the box office.

She keys it open then unlocks the safe. She has second
thoughts and removes half the cash from the bank bag.
On her way out she closes the door sharply – causing
something to fall and drawing OSSIPON attention to
where it thuds to the ground –

                    OSSIPON
                    (Sees)
Verloc –
                    (Turns to Winnie)
What are you up to? You have trapped me with
your money – for the Police –

                    WINNIE
I killed him.

                    OSSIPON
You?

                    WINNIE
He killed my son.

                    OSSIPON
That is awful.
                    (Beat)
Now I understand.

WINNIE
We have to go! Now Tom, now!

OSSIPON
(Quiet)
This is what we are going to do. We are going
to catch a train. Tonight. You're going to close
the cinema in twenty minutes as always. No
one will notice until tomorrow night when the
cinema does not open. Do you understand?

WINNIE
Yes.

OSSIPON
Good.
    I will go to the station now to buy
the tickets – but international tickets are
expensive –

WINNIE
(Shoving the bag at him)
Here. Take the money.

OSSIPON
I will be careful with this.
    (He slips the bag under his jacket. Winnie
    dodges his attempt to steal a goodbye kiss)
Twenty minutes –

WINNIE
Hurry back!

OSSIPON
And hide the body –

He slips away.

EXT. CINEMA STREET — NIGHT.

OSSIPON calmly walks away from the cinema.
He begins to walk quickly – smiling. He begins to
run – laughing. At the corner and immediately bumps
into CONSTABLE 1 causing the bank bag to fall.

> CONSTABLE 1
> (Picking it up)
> Where did you get this Mr Ossipon?

> OSSIPON
> You know me?

> CONSTABLE 1
> Obviously.

> OSSIPON
> (Inadvertently looking back at the cinema)
> Then you know that I edit a newspaper. Those
> are propaganda funds.

> CONSTABLE 1
> (Off the tell)
> Let's go back to the theatre and see if anybody's
> lost anything.

> OSSIPON
> But why? That's my money! Let go of me!
> I haven't been there!

CONSTABLE 1 leads the way.

OSSIPON (CONT'D)
You're making a mistake! I've done nothing
wrong!

CONSTABLE I
Let's just see what Mr Verloc has to say —

OSSIPON
You know Verloc?

CONSTABLE I
I know everyone around here.
(Firmly)
C'mon —

OSSIPON
It's all a big misunderstanding —

INT. CINEMA LOBBY — NIGHT.

OSSIPON
(Pushed inside)
I haven't been near this place in a month.

CONSTABLE I
Is that so?
(He rings the bell, then notices Winnie)
Ma'am has this man done anything to you?

She begins to cry —

OSSIPON
I have done nothing wrong. I was running for
my life — she is crazy!

CONSTABLE 1
(Approaches the lobby with Ossipon in tow)
Stop squirming!

OSSIPON
Let me out of here! She's crazy.

CONSTABLE 1
(Sees Verloc's corpse)
This just got interesting —

OSSIPON
She did it! I was terrified. I was running away
from her!

CONSTABLE 1
Shut up.
(He picks up the phone and dials)
Constable Costa here. I need Inspector Heat
immediately at Rua do Loreto 12. Rua do
Loreto 12.

BLACK.

EXT. CINEMA STREET — NIGHT.

HEAT gets out of his car and notices WINNIE being put
into a police car by CONSTABLE 1. He approaches then
is stopped by the sense that someone is nearby. He turns
to face —

PROFESSOR
I didn't expect to see you here tonight
Inspector. It must be well past you bed time.

HEAT
(Turns away, walking)
I didn't expect to see you either. You had a lot
to do with what has happened today. Proud of
yourself?

PROFESSOR
Proud. Me? I feel no pride. I feel no shame.
I have no master —
        (Sees WINNIE when the "Nivea"
        [blue and white police car] passes)
Is that Verloc's wife?

HEAT
That is a very sad woman.

PROFESSOR
What have you done with his remains?

HEAT
You can go inside and see for yourself — He's in
the lobby lying in a pool of his own blood.

PROFESSOR
Verloc? Wasn't he blown up?
        Don't explain. Someone killed him.
An outlaw got his just deserts —

HEAT
No law can touch him now. And no one can
help his wife.

PROFESSOR
Don't waste any of your sentimentality on me
Inspector. What do I care? I'm just a starving

bomb maker. I have no future. I disdain the
future but I am a force. Why don't you arrest
me now?

                    HEAT
           (Walking up the stairs)
When the time comes —

               CONSTABLE II
Evening Inspector. There's already —

                    HEAT
                  (Angry)
Don't let that crowd contaminate the scene!
             (Turns to Professor)
Maybe a crowd will one day tear you to pieces —

                 PROFESSOR
(Watches Heat depart as people surround him)
Ah yes. The crowd. Filthy countless multitude.
Unconscious. Blind.
                  (Smiles)
Let them.

BLACK.

LOOP.

THE SECRET AGENT
2015

CAST

Mr. Verloc
Adrian Schiller

Winnie
Beatriz Batarda

Mr. Vladimir
William Tapley

Inspector Heat
Marcello Urgeghe

The Professor
Miguel Guilherme

Ossipon
Filipe Vargas

Michaelis
Pedro Lacerda

Yundt
Norman MacCallum

Assistant Commissioner
Gonçalo Waddington

Secretary of State
Albano Jerónimo

Functionary
Simão Cayatte

Secretary
Joana Cunha Ferreira

Constable
Carloto Cotta

Musicians
Paulo Furtado (guitar),
Filipe Costa (keyboards)

Extras
Adriano Monteiro,
Alberto Leitão, Alexandre
Farromba, Amílcar
Figueiredo, André
Butler, André Martins,
António Carpinteiro,
Antonio Ricardo, Artur
Castro, Artur Costa,
Bruno Soares, Carla
Silva, Carlos Abreu,
Carlos Correia, Cedrico
Vaz, Célia Rolo, Cristina
Pereira, Diogo Marques,
Ernesto Junior, Fábio
Miguel, Fátima Vaz,
Fernanda Dias, Fersan
Sambu, Francisco Santos,
Helena Gonçalves,
James Bell, Jan Palmeiro,
João Figueiredo, Jorge
Bandeira, Jorge das
Neves, Jorge Guilherme,

Jorge Teixeira, Luís Pires,
Luís Sousa, Luísa Simões,
Lurdes Silva, Manuel
Antunes, Manuel Mendes
Santos, Manuel Simões,
Marcelo Castro, Nuno
Nita, Patrick Mendes,
Paulo Junqueiro, Pedro
Crespo, Rafael Lima,
Ricardo Lopes, Rui Dias,
Sónia Ferreira, Teresa
Boanova Silva, Teresa
Tavares, Vanda Pereira,
Vasco Assunção,
Vinícius Silva

CREW

Writer, director, editor
Stan Douglas

1st director assistant
Bruno Lourenço

2nd director assistant
Patrick Mendes

*Casting director
(Portugal)*
Raquel da Silva

*Casting director
(UK)*
Sophie Parrot

Executive producers
David Zwirner,
Stan Douglas

Producer
Luís Urbano

Production coordinator
Cristina Almeida

Production manager
Emídio Miguel

Unit manager
João Gusmão

Production secretary
Catarina Norberto

1st production assistant
Miguel Perdigão;
David Zwirner gallery:
Justine Durett;
Stan Douglas studio:
Linda Chinfen

Production assistant
João Manso

Production assistant
Marta Montalvão

*Production assistant
(extra day)*
Bruno Pinheiro

*Production assistants
(extra day)*
Susana Lopes,
Hugo Pinto

Director of photography
Leonardo Simões

1st camera assistant
Hugo Azevedo

*1st camera assistant
Camera B*
Miguel Malheiros

*1st camera assistant
Camera B*
Danilo Bernardes
de Souza

2nd camera assistant
Ricardo Simões

2nd camera assistant
Inês Gonçalo

*2nd camera assistant
(extra day)*
Soraia Rêgo

DIT
José Pedroso

Drone pilot
António Simões

Drone image assistant
David Vasques

Gaffer
Mário Soares

Best boys
Bruno Lopes, Artur
Andrade, João Silva

Key grip
Manuel Ramos

Grip
Tiago Valente

Genny operator
João Caires

Sound recordist
Vasco Pimentel

*Sound recordist
(extra day)*
Copi

Boom operator
Michelle Chan

*Tiger Man studio
engineers*
Bandido Sessions
(Pedro Borges,
Tiago André,
Frederico Gracias)

Foley artists
Don Harrison,
Ian Mackie

Foley recordist
Rick Senechal

Sound effects editor
Adam Fulton

Production designer
Bruno Duarte

Art director
Cypress Cook

Set dresser
Kid

*Assistant
production designer*
Susana Moura

Costume designer
Patrícia Dória

*Wardrobe
assistant*
Regina Morais

Make-up artist
Íris Peleira

Make-up assistant
Mariana Mattos

Hair stylist
Sandra Meleiro

Hair assistant
Márcia Lourenço

Trainees
Sael Bartolucci,
Yusuke Ito

Catering
Vl Expresso Catering

Colourist
Dermot Shane

*Sound supervisor and
installation technician*
Brodie Smith

*Programmer and
video technician*
Peter Courtemanche

ACKNOWLEDGEMENTS

Câmara Municipal
    de Lisboa
Lisboa Film Commission
Polícia de Segurança
    Pública
Cinemateca Portuguesa
EGEAC/ Cinema
    São Jorge

ACKNOWLEDGEMENTS

Many people generously availed
themselves for collaboration in this
research or to testify in the making
The Secret Agent and *Disco Angola*.
Margarida Pais, Filipa Sanchez,
Ivo André Braz, Ana Sá Fernandes,
Fernanda Rollo, Irene Pimentel and
Dulce Maria Reis all deserve hearty
acknowledgement for their engage-
ment with this project.

The production of the exhibition
Interregnum, in Lisbon, that this book
accompanies was meticulously realised by the Museu Coleção Berardo
team, coordinated by Rita Lougares,
and of the book itself by Nuno Ferreira
de Carvalho.

Our profound gratitude also
goes to David Zwirner, Angela Choon,
Justine Durret, Erin Hennessy,
Alexandra Willkie, Stephanie
Stockbridge and Stephanie Daniel of
the David Zwirner gallery, and to Erin
Manns and Emma Mee of the Victoria
Miro gallery. Their assiduity was
indispensable in the realisation of this
exhibition. We also offer our sincere
thanks to the Goetz Collection the
loan of works for the exhibition at the
Museu Coleção Berardo, in Lisbon.

The team at Stan Douglas's
studio was unsurpassable in the care
and versatility they lavished upon
the adaptation of the works to new
exhibition spaces. To Linda Chinfen
and Brodie Smith we express our
warm thanks.

But it is, above all, to Stan
Douglas – who continues to amaze
with his fascinating work, ever
problematising the status of the art
object – that we wish to express
our most heartfelt appreciation and
greatest admiration.

Pedro Lapa
Artistic director
Museu Coleção Berardo

STAN DOUGLAS.
INTERREGNUM

Museu Coleção Berardo, Lisboa
21 October 2015 – 14 February 2016

Curator
Pedro Lapa

Production
Rita Lougares

Registration
António Pedro Mendes

Education department
Cristina Gameiro, coordenation

Editorial coordination
Nuno Ferreira de Carvalho

Press office
Namalimba Coelho

Production assistance
Frederico Albuquerque Mendes

Support
Stan Douglas studio
David Zwirner gallery
Victoria Miro gallery

HISTORY AND
INTERREGNUM.
THREE WORKS
BY STAN DOUGLAS

Edited by
Pedro Lapa

Authors
Pedro Lapa
Stan Douglas

Editorial coordination
Nuno Ferreira de Carvalho

Graphic design
Raquel Pinto

Translation
Ruth Rosengarten

Copy-editing and proofing
Nuno Ferreira de Carvalho

Prepress, printing and binding
Gráfica Maiadouro

500 copies

ISBN
978-3-943620-38-2
Archive Books
978-989-8239-48-8
Museu Coleção Berardo

Legal deposit 399808/15

Archive Books
Dieffenbachstraße 31
10967 Berlin
mail@archivebooks.org
www.archivebooks.org

Museu Coleção Berardo
Praça do Império
1449-003 Lisboa, Portugal
+351 21 361 28 78
museuberardo@museuberardo.pt
www.museuberardo.pt

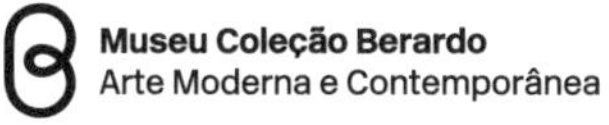

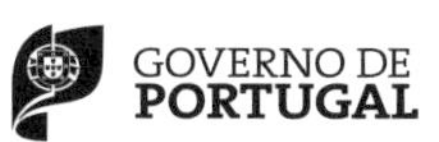

Sponsor:
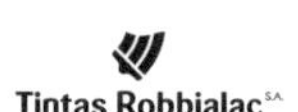

Support:
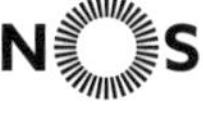

*Free admission
supported by:* **Associação
de Colecções**

Exhibition support:
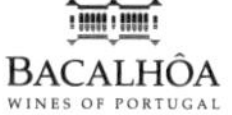